Real Girls:

Shifting Perceptions on

Identity, Relationships,

and the Media

I0134599

Kiana Clayborn, LMSW

Jessica Traylor, Ed.S.

Cover art by Daniel Sergent, M.Ed.

Printed in the United States of America

ISBN: 0615399886

Unless otherwise noted, Scripture quotations are from the Holy Bible, New International Version, copyright © 1973, 1978, 1984 by International Bible Society.

Visit us at http://www.realgirls.us

Email the authors at contact@realgirls.us

Dedication

Real Girls was birthed from the power and strength of girls across the world. We, the authors, applaud you for your spirit and determination.

Thank you!

Comments from past participants:

I learned...

- You should always be you and live in reality.
- You should do what you love and don't let anyone take that away from you.
- No one can make you do anything that you don't want to do because you have a powerful mind of your own.
- The best way to express yourself is to be you. You shouldn't want to be like someone else, you should want to be you.
- Different types of relationships (healthy and unhealthy).
- Models in magazines are airbrushed.
- Try to show the real you. Love who you are.

General Comments

- I liked talking about music lyrics and magazines.
- I liked being in a girls-only group because you can open up more than when guys are around.
- Be a real girl! Eat an Oreo!!
- Real girls can do anything.

CONTENTS

Introduction

We are facing a major crisis in our world today that is not like anything we've ever seen. Yes, we are currently experiencing an economic down turn, as we hear and see daily on the news reports. We are in a time like no other, when we are continually faced with natural disasters, as noted by the recent earthquake that devastated Haiti. Obvious crises are all around us and we can't escape them; however, the most deadly and subtle crisis is the state of girls in our country.

Research shows that girls struggle with identity development and low self-concept in record breaking numbers, compared to boys (American Psychological Association, Task Force on the Sexualization of Girls, 2007; The Dove Self-Esteem Fund, 2008; Girls, Inc., 2002). According to The Dove Self-Esteem Fund (2008), ***seven in ten girls believe they are not good enough or do not measure up in some way***, including their looks, performance in school and relationships with their friends and family members. This means that over half of our young girls feel inadequate, unworthy, inferior, and/or hopeless.

As a nation and community, we must begin to address this crisis and provide hope for girls of today so that they can become women of tomorrow. *Real Girls* is a practical guide for anyone who works with young girls and has a passion to empower them to reach their fullest potential.

As Christians, we (the authors) believe that it is our duty to help those in need. Based on the current condition of youth, particularly young girls in our society, we must now more than ever exercise our Christian faith and be a beacon of light to our young girls. It is our hope that after reading this book you will become a "true" change agent in the life of a young girl, guiding her on the journey from youth to womanhood.

This book includes an eight session outline, which is designed to assist middle and high school age girls to develop a ***realistic self-concept, media literacy skills, and communication skills, while also learning about healthy behaviors and positive relationships.*** As each participant goes through the program their identity begins to be shaped, as their perceptions about self-concept, media, and relationships are slowly shifted to more realistic, positive frameworks.

Each session has correlating Christian biblical scriptures, which provide a Christian perspective and foundation for the topics in each session. Facilitators can choose whether or not to incorporate the scriptures, based on each individual setting. The eight sessions are:

Session 1) Real Me

Session 2) Media Messages

Session 3) Musical Messages

Session 4) Media Stereotypes

Session 5) Real Talk

Session 6) Real Power

Session 7) Healthy Relationships

Session 8) Digital Me/Collage

The information and resources in this book can be applied to various settings such as community youth development organizations, church youth groups, mental health agencies, and schools. Community youth development organizations, mental health agencies, and schools can best use this guide by working through the eight session outline, along with the resources and appendix. Church youth group leaders are encouraged to combine the session outlines with the additional information provided in the Church Youth Group Guide found on pages 85-89. Parents are encouraged to use the session outlines as a starting point for communicating effectively with their daughters.

Identity Development

As we begin to address the issues of identity development, self-concept and relationships among girls, we must take a deeper look at the media and its influence in our culture today. In today's world technology and the media have become a part of our everyday life. It is quite rare to see someone in today's culture that is truly independent of media and technology, someone who does not use any form of technology on a daily basis. Media and technology go hand in hand; it seems that one cannot exist without the other, much like our culture would not be the same without the two.

Media provides a social outlet, which connects us to the world around us. From the media we gain a sense of who we are in relation to the culture in which we live. The media, along with other factors, dictates our relationships and qualifies what is normal vs. abnormal. Media influences our values and choices, down to which car we will drive and the type of clothing we will wear. According to Girls Inc. (2002), "it is estimated that girls typically viewed more than 40,000 TV ads per year in the early 90s". One can only assume that this number has increased greatly over time.

Recognizing now that seven in ten girls struggle with self-esteem issues, it is also critical to add that these same girls are being bombarded with media influences through TV ads. Again, we see that media holds a major place in our culture and it often shapes how we think and most importantly how we behave. Understanding media will enable us to better address girls and their struggles with identity development, self-concept and relationships.

Identity development is critical in addressing the needs of girls who face issues of low self-esteem, patterns of unhealthy relationships, and overall negative self-perception. We reference Erik Erikson's Eight Stages of Development, with a focus on stage five. The Eight Stages of Development are:

1) Trust vs. Mistrust

2) Autonomy vs. Shame

3) Initiative vs. Guilt

4) Industry vs. Inferiority

5) Identity vs. Identity Confusion

6) Intimacy vs. Isolation

7) Generativity vs. Stagnation

8) Integrity vs. Despair

Stage one is primarily concerned with developing a sense of trust in the environment, particularly the caregivers, to provide what is needed by the infant. During stage two the toddler works to learn about the environment and control her bodily functions (walking, talking, toilet training, etc.). Stage three, which incorporates pre-school age, children are focused on demonstrating their ability to create or initiate activities. School-age children attempt to develop a sense of self-worth by mastering skills during stage four.

The stage of development that impacts adolescents ages 12-19 is stage 5: Identity vs. Identity Confusion. In this stage adolescents are "finding themselves;" exploration of who they are and what their purpose is becomes the major question in their lives.

When working with girls who are constantly flooded with societal messages from the media, peers, and other social sources, it becomes clear that issues of low self-image and negative self-perception may result. Girls who constantly try to live up to the impossible ideals received from society will inevitably be let down and feel that they are unworthy of acceptance.

The development of a positive, realistic identity is necessary in order to successfully navigate the next stage of development, Intimacy vs. Isolation. With a positive resolution to the identity crisis, adolescents are able to form healthy intimate relationships with friends and family members. These more intimate types of relationships are based on a true understanding of their self-concept and their place in the world. When the identity development stage is left without true resolution, adolescents are unsure of who they are in relation to others and in relation to the world in general. This identity confusion leads to issues of low self-image and negative self-perception that have been shown to be related to higher incidences of self-destructive behavior (Dove Self-Esteem Fund, 2008).

Real Girls is designed to help with identity development. Once girls are aware of who they are, beyond society's messages, they are able to resolve the identity stage of development. Having a true sense of self will support girls in exploring healthy relationships.

Youth Development

In order to gain a better understanding of youth development programs, and how they apply to working with youth, it is important to first, recognize the basic tenants of effective youth development programs. According to a study conducted by the University of Washington, School of Social Work (1998) entitled "Positive Youth Development in the United States," youth development programs should promote bonding, foster resilience, and foster clear and positive identity. These are just a few basic foundational principles of youth development programs.

An important aspect of youth development programs is bonding. Bonding occurs when an emotional attachment is formed between a child and a specific individual and/or group. It is important for children to have the opportunity to make secure attachments in life, as this will impact their future outcome. Youth without secure attachments will have difficulty forming healthy relationships.

Resilience is often described as the ability to "bounce back" from any adverse life condition. ***Resilience is defined as patterns that protect children from adopting problem behaviors in the face of risk.*** Building resilience in youth is critical to their success as adults.

Fostering a clear and positive identity among youth is another major component of successful youth development programs. Identity development for youth is crucial as they attempt to navigate their way through the social maze of life. It is at the identity development stage that identity confusion can occur. Once a youth develops a clear concept of who they are, they will be less likely to suffer with issues of low self-esteem and engage in self-destructive behaviors, such as using substances, participating in risky sexual activities, and developing unhealthy relationships.

The *Real Girls* curriculum addresses the previously mentioned foundational principles of a successful youth development program. It provides girls with social support through an all girl group setting. This type of environment can allow each girl the opportunity to experience a sense of belonging and connectedness. Through interactive and engaging skill building activities in each *Real Girls* session, participants are provided with opportunities to experience success, which can promote individual resiliency. As each participant goes through the program their identity begins to be shaped, as their perceptions about self-concept, media, and relationships are slowly shifted to more realistic, positive frameworks.

Group Process

In working with young girls, group work has often been recognized as a positive and successful means of engagement. Group work and/or group process has been used in the field of Social Work practice and mental health programs for more than 30 years. A National Association of Social Work (1985) report on the effectiveness of social work practice in mental health programs analyzed 142 studies and found the use of group process the third most frequently used among 26 intervention techniques.

Group process is successful for several reasons, particularly as it relates to working with youth. Youth by nature learn through hands-on activities and are natural leaders. Group process allows the facilitator to be a guide to the group rather than the leader of the group, which encourages youth leaders in the group to naturally emerge. A successful group facilitator allows groups to organize themselves and does not get in the way of the natural group process. Young girls naturally thrive in this type of setting because they are viewed as a vital part of the process and are not seen as pawns to be moved.

When understanding the low self-concept issues that several young girls face, it becomes clearer that group process may assist young girls in slowly finding the voice that lies within them. According to a national survey compiled in Choosing Community: Girls Get Together to Be Themselves from Girls, Inc. (2002) "Two-thirds of students (67%) believe that girls are more likely to say what they really feel in groups with only girls". It is also important to note that "those who feel connected are less likely to engage in high-risk behavior"

(Malekoff, 2004).This illustrates another example of the effect that peer groups can have in the life of a young girl.

The type of group process utilized in *Real Girls* is the free form style. The free form group allows group members to exchange in dialogue freely with other group members, as it relates to the group theme. The role of the facilitator in this type of group is to provide the group with basic foundational principles, such as respecting others, listening to others, and group member responsibility. This group process style is most successful when group members become familiar with each other and recognize their vested responsibility in the group. The free form group process allows each participant to bring their individual and unique characteristics to the group. This produces a more dynamic and engaging group.

Although, the role of the group facilitator is used primarily to guide the group as it forms, the facilitator also sets the tone for the development of group rules, which the group ultimately decides. When facilitating groups it is critical that group rules be established early. Implementing group rules provides the group with the appropriate structure needed to explore and engage in the group process. Listed are sample group rules that may be used when conducting the *Real Girls* sessions:

1) Respect others
2) Confidentiality (What is said in group stays in the group)
3) Agree to Disagree
4) Be an Active Participant

Preserving the confidentiality of group members is extremely important in maintaining the integrity of the group process. This should be stressed with all group members; however, the facilitator should indicate their responsibility in reporting information to appropriate authorities if a participant shares information that could be harmful to themselves and/or someone else.

It is important to understand the stages of group development, in order to effectively facilitate groups. The five stages of group development, according to Tuckman and Jensen (1977), are: 1) Forming, 2) Storming, 3) Norming, 4) Performing, and 5) Adjourning. During the forming stage group membership is not fully understood and youth require guidance and direction from the facilitator. At this stage it is common for group members to appear less engaged and uninterested in the group process (don't worry; this is all a part of the process). In the Storming stage group members are still searching for their purpose. Power struggles may develop during this stage as group members begin to examine their place in the group process. This is a natural process for the group; the facilitator should expect feelings of uncertainty and slight discomfort from group members (remember to stay the course and not get discouraged).

The Norming stage is important in the transformation of the group because cohesiveness emerges during this stage. Group members become more active and engaged participants. The facilitator's role becomes more of an observer, while the group slowly begins to become independent.

The next stage in the group process is the Performing stage. During this stage group members now have a solid direction and a shared vision. Group members begin to take on a more intense leadership role concerning group activities and begin to execute tasks. The Facilitator is a true facilitator at this point, allowing the group to emerge as active, vested participants.

The final stage is Adjourning. This is when the group finalizes their tasks and celebrates their accomplishments. This may be a time of sadness for some who have developed a connection to the group. It is important to be sensitive to the feelings of all group members during this time. Closure activities, such as discussing the group process, strengths, and weaknesses, may help group members move through this stage more easily.

Stages of Group Development

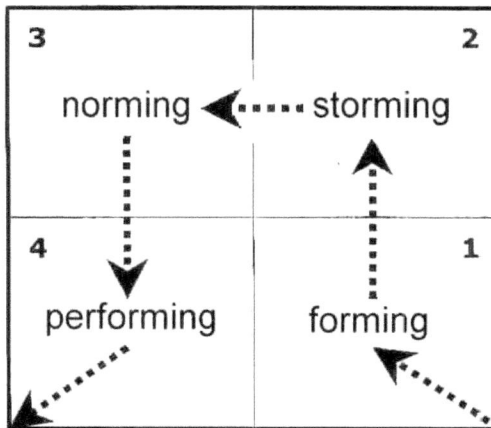

```
3                            2

   norming ◄·····storming

              ▲

4                            1

   performing      forming
```

Educational Standards

Real Girls is aligned to educational standards, including the Common Core Standards and individual state standards. A rubric is provided to assist with assessment.

<u>Common Core State Standards</u>

Language (6th-12th)

- Students will apply knowledge of language to understand how language functions in different contexts, to make effective choices for meaning or style, and to comprehend more fully when reading or listening.

- Students will demonstrate understanding of word relationships and nuances in word meanings.

Writing (6th-12th)

- Students will use technology, including the Internet, to produce and publish writing and to interact and collaborate with others.

- Students will gather relevant information from multiple print and digital sources, assess the credibility and accuracy of each source, and integrate the information while avoiding plagiarism.

Reading (6th-12th)

- Students will interpret words and phrases as they are used in a text, including determining technical, connotative, and figurative meanings, and analyze how specific word choices shape meaning or tone.

- Students will assess how point of view or purpose shapes the content and style of a text.

- Students will integrate and evaluated content presented in diverse formats and media, including visually and quantitatively, as well as in words.

Speaking and Listening (6th-12th)

- Students will prepare for and participate effectively in a range of conversations and collaborations with diverse partners, building on others' ideas and expressing their own clearly and persuasively.

- Students will integrate and evaluate information presented in diverse media formats, including visually, quantitatively, and orally.

- Students will evaluate a speaker's point of view, reasoning, and use of evidence and rhetoric.

- Students will make strategic use of digital media and visual displays of data to express information and enhance understanding of presentations.

Georgia Performance Standards

ELA6W3 - The student uses research and technology to support writing.

ELA6LSV1 - The student participates in student-to-teacher, student-to-student, and group verbal interactions.

ELA6LSV2 - The student listens to and views various forms of text and media in order to gather and share information, persuade others, and express and understand ideas. The student will select and critically analyze messages using rubrics as assessment tools.

Information Processing Skills

- Identify issues and/or problems and alternative solutions
- Distinguish between fact and opinion
- Draw conclusions and make generalizations
- Determine adequacy and/or relevancy of information
- Check for consistency of information
- Interpret political cartoons

Assessment

A rubric is provided, in Appendix B, to assess participants' progress on critically analyzing activities and expressing a deepening level of self-reflection.

Real Girls

8 Session Outline

Objective: This program was designed to help middle and high school girls develop effective self-concept, media literacy, and communication skills, while learning about healthy behaviors and positive relationships.

Process: Girls will meet in a small group once a week for 45-60 minutes. They will engage in small group discussion, media analysis, self-reflection, and role play. Each girl will produce a digital story or photo collage about "real girls."

Materials: Each girl will need a spiral or composition notebook. Girls will experience various media through the use of editorial magazines, advertisements, videos, and music. It will be necessary to gather and review relevant media samples. Resources are provided at the end of the book to assist with obtaining media samples. Additionally, access to Audio/video equipment, computers, internet, chart paper, markers, and pens/pencils will be needed.

Topics:
Session 1 – Real Me

Session 2 – Media Messages

Session 3 – Musical Messages

Session 4 – Media Stereotypes

Session 5 – Real Talk

Session 6 – Real Power

Session 7 – Healthy Relationships

Session 8 – Digital Me/Collage

Real Me

Session One

The primary focus of this eight-session group discussion guide is to assist girls, and the adults who care about them, talk about sensitive issues, such as...

1. Who are you?
2. Who does the mass media say you should be?
3. How do your self-concept and media awareness impact your relationships and choices?

As we answer these questions, and many others, we will work from a foundation of solid research, timeless truth, and common sense.

This first lesson begins the discussion of developing a realistic, positive self-concept. ***Self-concept refers to how we view ourselves in relation to the world around us.*** Sometimes young women develop a negative self-concept, thinking they are not as good as others. Sometimes young women develop an inflated self-concept, thinking they are better than others. A positive, balanced self-concept will allow young women to acknowledge their strengths and weaknesses. Participation in girls' groups has been shown to foster leadership development and open communication, while increasing educational expectations (Girls, Inc., 2002).

In order to discuss how girls' identity develops, they must understand the impact of media on their lives. Media can include television shows, magazines, Internet websites, music, video games, billboards, clothing store models, print and video ads, and movies. Many of the media portrayals of girls show them in limited roles focused on superficial beauty. Research shows that **unrealistic notions of female beauty and body shapes and limited gender stereotypes negatively affect young women** (APA Task Force on the Sexualization of Girls, 2007).

Additionally, girls' relationships are intimately connected to how they feel about themselves. One in four girls in high school was in a physical fight in the last year (Girls, Inc., 2008). One in four youth reports verbal, physical, emotional, or sexual abuse each year (Centers for Disease Control and Prevention, 2006). With these high numbers of abuse incidents, it is no surprise that we have more girls engaging in binge drinking, suicide attempts, and sexual activity. Rates of drug, alcohol, and tobacco use are more than twice as high in girls who report physical or sexual dating abuse than in girls who report no abuse (Centers for Disease Control and Prevention, 2006). In order to combat these statistics, our **girls need to learn how to communicate effectively and identify the warning signs of an unhealthy relationship**.

Real Me

1. Introduction to *Real Girls*
   a. Introduce the topics of self-concept, media awareness, and healthy relationships
   b. Determine group rules
   c. Discuss confidentiality
   d. Have each girl complete the survey – appendix A
2. True or not true?
   a. Each girl comes up with two statements about herself: one true and one false
   b. After a girl shares her statements the group should guess which one is true
3. Video Discussion: Akeelah and the Bee – Deepest Fear
4. The best things about me
   a. Girls complete each statement in their notebooks
      i. I am good at...
      ii. What makes me special is...
5. Five things that matter most in a person
   a. Girls answer each question in their notebooks
      i. Write 5 things that matter most in a person.
      ii. Write 5 things that describe you.
      iii. How are these two lists similar or different?

6. Love me not? Love me!

    a. Complete the **Love the real me, or not?** worksheet – appendix C

    b. Discuss some of your answers with the group

7. Closing

    a. Name one thing you learned about someone else

    b. Name one thing you learned about yourself

8. Facilitator's Reflection

    a. Use the two page **Facilitator's Notes** to guide your reflections on this session

    b. Use the rubric to assess each girl's level of participation

Media Resources

Video

Akeelah and the Bee – Deepest Fear (www.wingclips.com)
- Dr. Larabee forces Akeelah to read an inspirational quote and then explain what it means to her.
- Discuss: What does this scene mean to you? Why would some people be afraid to succeed?

Phoebe in Wonderland – I'm Scared (www.wingclips.com)
- Phoebe learns from Miss Dodger that one day she will come to accept and love her individuality.
- Discuss: What does this scene mean to you? Is there something about you that makes you different or special? What does it mean to love your self? Why do you think Phoebe says she is scared?

Nanny Diaries – Who Am I? (www.wingclips.com)
- While in an important job interview, Annie can't find the answer the most basic question: Who is Annie Braddock?
- Discuss: Why is it important to know who you are? Who or what tells you who you are? How do you know which messages are correct?

Scripture

Philippians 2:15 – so that you may become blameless and pure, children of God without fault in a crooked and depraved generation, in which you shine like stars in the universe

Jeremiah 1:5 - Before I formed you in the womb I knew you, before you were born I set you apart

1st Peter2:9 - But you are a chosen generation, a royal priesthood, a holy nation, a peculiar people.

Audio

"Beautiful" and "Fighter" by Christina Aguilera

"Just a Girl" by No Doubt

"I Am Not My Hair" and "Beautiful Flower" by India Arie

"The Climb" by Miley Cyrus

"Ordinary Girl" by Miley Cyrus

"Six Feet Tall" by Never Say Never

Internet

- www.wingclips.com – Movie clips organized by topic
- www.lyricsmania.com – Music lyrics organized by artist

Facilitator's Notes

Session One – Real Me

How did your group respond to establishing ground rules and discussing confidentiality? What ideas do you have for interesting ways to approach group rules in the future?

_____

_____

_____

_____

How did your group respond to the opening activity? How can you use opening activities to set the tone for your groups? What ideas do you have for future activities?

_____

_____

_____

_____

What sort of comments did your group make during the video discussion? What ideas do you have for future discussion questions?

_____

_____

_____

_____

_____

Did your girls have any difficulty completing the survey? How can you use the results to make future sessions more relevant? What ideas do you have for modifying the survey in the future?

_____

_____

_____

_____

What concerns do you have about the group process? How will you resolve these concerns?

_____

_____

_____

_____

Is there anything you will do differently the next time you teach this specific session?

_____

_____

_____

_____

Additional thoughts:

_____

_____

_____

_____

_____

_____

Media Messages

Session Two

According to the Kaiser Family Foundation (2010), media use by youth ages 8-18 has increased to almost eight hours a day. The majority of that time is spent watching television (4.5 hours), listening to music (2.5 hours), and using the computer (1.5 hours). The use of print media has decreased to almost a half hour each day. In this digital age, we need to expand our definitions of "text" and "reading" to include the numerous messages received from sources other than traditional print media.

Young girls spend a large part of their waking hours consuming messages from the media about how they should look, dress, think, and behave. While some of these messages are positive, the harmful messages seem to overpower the helpful messages. ***Repeated exposure to unrealistic notions of female beauty and body shapes, along with limited gender stereotypes, may result in young girls internalizing these standards***.

According to Fabrianesi, Jones, and Reid (2008), there is little difference between pre-adolescent girls' magazines and adolescent girls' magazines. They found that the age of models in both magazines were inappropriate (average age 24). Further, these models had a public history of being involved in disordered eating and drug use.

This session is designed to encourage girls to explore the images they see in magazines and on television to determine the true purpose of their creation. Girls are guided through a series of questions to expand their ability to identify that *media images are created for a specific audience, with the specific intent of selling a message or product*. The activities include analysis of a magazine advertisement and a television show.

During this stage of identity development girls can learn to handle complex abstract ideas. Talking about these issues in the context of an all girls group will allow them to be more open and honest in their communication. Girls can learn to develop their own standards of beauty and future expectations, based on reality rather than the media.

It is not the intent of this session or curriculum to encourage girls to be cynical or to encourage them to withdraw from the world. Rather, the intent is to foster critical reflection which leads to action. Girls are encouraged to *take an active role in interpreting the meaning of mediated standards of beauty while discovering their own inner beauty*. They are guided through the process of determining how they will respond to messages and images that do not fit with their own reality or the reality of the people around them.

Media Messages

1. Magazine Analysis

    a. Divide into groups of two or three

    b. Give each group a common teen magazine or allow them to use the Internet to find a website associated with a common teen magazine

    c. Each group should look at the magazine and discuss the content (articles, pictures, advertisements, etc.)

    d. Each girl should record the following in her notebook

        i.   Types of articles and advertisements

        ii.   Based on these articles and advertisements, what should girls be interested in and work toward accomplishing?

        iii. What do these articles and advertisements imply about girls?

        iv. What impact do these types of media messages have on girls? Society?

        v.   Your viewpoint

    e. Each group explains their magazine to the large group

2. "Evolution" Video

    a. Show the "Evolution" Video
http://www.studio2b.org/lounge/games/uniquelyMe/main.html

b. After watching the video, girls should discuss their thoughts about the reality of what is shown in advertisements

c. Have girls share one of their thoughts about the video

3. Video Discussion: Penelope – Not Your Nose

4. Theme Song Intro - homework

c. Introduce the homework of finding a personal theme song, including meaning, personal insight, and background

d. Play a few songs with positive girl messages

a. Discuss how the songs relate to girls' experiences

5. Closing

a. Name one thing you learned about someone else

b. Name one thing you learned about yourself

6. Facilitator's Reflection

a. Use the two page **Facilitator's Notes** to guide your reflections on this session

b. Use the rubric to assess each girl's level of participation

Media Resources

Session Two – Media Messages

Video

Evolution

(http://www.studio2b.org/lounge/games/uniquelyMe/main.html)

- The video shows the change in a girl's appearance from the beginning of a photo shoot, through make up, lighting changes, and air brushing.
- Discuss: What did you find interesting about this video? What does this make you think about the images you see in magazines and on television?

Penelope – Not Your Nose (www.wingclips.com)

- Penelope and her mother discuss how the imperfection that is her nose affects the possibility of finding a boyfriend.
- Discuss: What does this scene mean to you? Where do our ideas of beauty come from? What is real beauty? Is there any part of your body that you would like to change?

Scripture

Deuteronomy 4:16 – so that you do not become corrupt and make for yourselves an idol, an image of any shape, whether formed like a man or a woman

Deuteronomy 7:25 – The images of their gods you are to burn in the fire. Do not covet the silver and gold on them, and do not take it for yourselves, or you will be ensnared by it, for it is detestable to the LORD your God.

Daniel chapter 3 – King Nebuchadnezzar demands that all people bow down to the golden image he has created. Three Jewish men refuse to obey this command. They are thrown in the fiery furnace and rescued by God.

Audio

"Barbie Girl" by Aqua

"Lessons Learned" by Carrie Underwood

Internet

- www.about-face.org – Advertising about girls and women
- www.wingclips.com – Movie clips organized by topic
- www.medialit.org – Center for Media Literacy

Facilitator's Notes

Session Two – Media Messages

How did your group respond to the magazine analysis activity? How can you encourage more in depth analysis? Will you do anything differently in the future?

_____

_____

_____

How did your group respond to the Evolution video? What ideas do you have for other interesting video clips or advertisements that engage group members in discussion?

_____

_____

_____

What sort of comments did your group make during the second video discussion? What ideas do you have for future discussion questions?

_____

_____

_____

_____

What sort of questions or concerns did your group have about the Theme Song homework? What ideas do you have to make it more meaningful for them?

_____

_____

_____

_____

What concerns do you have about the group process? How will you resolve these concerns? Are there any group members who are hindering progress of the whole group?

_____

_____

_____

_____

Is there anything you will do differently the next time you teach this specific session?

_____

_____

_____

_____

Additional thoughts:

_____

_____

_____

_____

_____

Musical Messages

Session Three

Youth development experts agree that peer approval and parent approval of drug and alcohol use increases the likelihood that adolescents will engage in these behaviors (Adolescent Substance Abuse Knowledge Base, 2007). The same is true for sexual activity, cutting, and eating disorders. This session was designed to ***combat the idea that these self-destructive behaviors are acceptable to most youth and adults, as depicted in popular music.***

Young girls today are bombarded with thousands of media messages each day. One in three popular songs contains explicit references to drug or alcohol use, according to a new report in The Archives of Pediatrics and Adolescent Medicine (Primack, Dalton, Carroll, Agarwal & Fine, 2008). This means that kids are receiving about 35 references to substance abuse for every hour of music they listen to. An estimated 75 percent of teens spend two or three hours a day downloading or listening to music online (Love, Inc., 2010). Considering this information, a majority of youth receive more than 100 messages every day about substance abuse.

The reality is that not all adolescents are engaged in self-destructive behaviors (Centers for Disease Control and Prevention, 2010). According to the Centers for Disease Control, Youth Risk Behavior Survey completed in 2009, 7% of students report frequently smoking cigarettes, 24% report binge drinking, 21% report using marijuana, 34% report currently being sexually active, and 44% report trying to lose weight. While these numbers are higher than we would like, they are a powerful message that the majority of young people are making positive decisions regarding their behavior.

In order to help young girls combat the influence of messages in music, they need to be taught how to critically analyze what they listen to. This is a more sensible alternative to censorship, knowing that we cannot prevent young people from listening to music, whether at home, at a friend's house, or on the Internet. With the tools in this session girls will learn about the power of words, the emotional impact of music, and how to analyze the meaning of song lyrics.

At the end of this session girls will be given the task of creating a digital story about their lives. Group facilitators should locate or create an example of a digital story before teaching this session. The Internet resources on page 29 can be used as a starting point for locating an example.

This experience of constructing a digital media project will teach them about the individual elements that are involved in media creation. The primary goal of the digital storytelling project is to foster self-reflection; however, a deeper understanding of media is an intentional byproduct.

Musical Messages

Session Three Outline

1. Video Discussion: Akeelah and the Bee – Words Change the World

2. Theme Song Project

    a. Play a few songs brought in by girls

    b. Ask girls for their analysis of the songs

    c. Girls should answer the following questions in their notebook

        i. Whose Theme Song had the most impact? Why?

        ii. What have you learned about your classmates?

        iii. What have you learned about yourself?

    d. Discuss the experience

3. Final Group Project: Girls have two options for completing the final project – Digital Me or Real Girls Collage

    a. Digital Me – Digital Storytelling Project

        i. Discuss the idea of a digital personal story, with an example

        ii. Provide the girls with the outline of required elements, encourage them to take notes in their notebook

            1. Past – family, events, experiences

            2. Present – outside, inside, strengths, weaknesses, interests, hobbies, favorites (movies, music, food, clothes, websites, television shows, games, etc.)

        3. Future – goals, dreams, education, family, job, vacations, income, housing, helping community

        4. Self-Reflection – What I've learned about friends, family, school, love, etc.

        5. Closing – how you want others to see you now

    iii.   Discuss uploading projects to the Internet

    iv.   Girls begin work on a written outline in their notebook

  b. Real Girls Collage

    i.   Discuss the option of creating a collage using magazine pictures that depict "real girls"

    ii.   If choosing this option, girls should begin bringing in magazines and/or magazine pictures that portray real girls doing things that are important to them

    iii.   During the course of the group sessions the girls will work to put these pictures on a collage

4. Closing

  a. Name one thing you learned about someone else

  b. Name one thing you learned about yourself

5. Facilitator's Reflection

  a. Use the two page **_Facilitator's Notes_** to guide your reflections on this session

  b. Use the rubric to assess each girl's level of participation

Media Resources

Video

Akeelah and the Bee – Words Change the World

(www.wingclips.com)

- Frustrated that her spelling coach is making her read essays instead of memorizing words, Akeelah learns that it is the power of the words that matter.

- Discuss: What does this scene mean to you? Why are the words that we hear or speak important? Do you believe that words can change the world?

Madea's Family Reunion – Where You're Going

(www.wingclips.com)

- After taking Madea's advice to study hard, Nikki is rewarded for her hard work with a "B' on her Algebra test.

- Discuss: What does this scene mean to you? How does your history impact your present and your future?

Scripture

<u>1 John 4:1</u> – Dear friends, do not believe every spirit, but test the spirits to see whether they are from God, because many false prophets have gone out into the world.

<u>Deuteronomy 32:28-29</u> – They are a nation without sense, there is no discernment in them. If only they were wise and would understand this and discern what their end will be.

<u>Hebrews 4:12</u> – For the word of God is living and active. Sharper than any double-edged sword, it penetrates even to dividing soul and spirit, joints and marrow; it judges the thoughts and attitudes of the heart.

<u>Proverbs 3:13</u> - Blessed is the man who finds wisdom, the man who gains understanding.

Audio

"I Am Not My Hair" by India Arie
"Ordinary Girl" by Miley Cyrus

Internet

- www.storycenter.org – Center for digital storytelling
- http://digitalstorytelling.coe.uh.edu/persona_reflection.html
  - Digital story examples

Facilitator's Notes

Session Three – Musical Messages

What sort of comments did your group make during the video discussion? What ideas do you have for future discussion questions?

_____

_____

_____

_____

Did most group members do the homework activity? What will you do to encourage them to complete group homework in the future?

_____

_____

_____

_____

What sort of comments did your group make during the Theme Song discussion? Which songs had the most impact? Are there any songs you will play in the future?

_____

_____

_____

_____

How did group members respond to the project assignment? Will you explain it differently in the future?

_____

_____

_____

_____

What concerns do you have about the group process? How will you resolve these concerns?

_____

_____

_____

_____

Is there anything you will do differently the next time you teach this specific session?

_____

_____

_____

_____

Additional thoughts:

_____

_____

_____

_____

_____

_____

_____

Media Stereotypes

Session Four

It does not take much effort to think of the way different groups of people are commonly portrayed on television. Women and girls are often portrayed as passive and powerless. They are usually shown in the house, laughing, talking, or watching what others are doing. Men and boys, on the other hand, are often portrayed as independent, active, and powerful. They are usually shown outside, building things, fixing things, or fighting.

One glance around any community will demonstrate that these stereotypes are far from the truth. There are women in every sector of society, every career, and most levels of government. There are men who stay at home with the children and would not know how to begin to build or fixing anything. Today's girls need to know that these and other **stereotypes are based on the media's need to sell images and products**.

The standard of female beauty portrayed in the media is that of a young, thin, and white (or light skinned) girl. For most females, this image is unattainable without the use of diet aids, cosmetics, and other more drastic products or services. Unfortunately, girls who entertain this ideal of beauty are more likely to have low self-esteem, eating disorders, and unhealthy relationships.

This session is designed to demonstrate the way the mass media uses common stereotypes to shape our view of reality. Girls are encouraged to watch a television show with the intention of looking for stereotyped characters. While discussing these stereotypes, girls will be guided through a series of questions about how ***our attitudes and beliefs can be shaped by media messages***.

Additionally, stereotypical portrayals of people who are disabled or black are also common in the media. Disabled people are often shown to be helpless victims or heroes who overcome some obstacle. Black people are more likely than white people to be shown in lower paying jobs with unstable families. While it is not the intention of this session to focus on racism and discrimination, girls will be guided through discussions of how these issues are displayed in the media.

Girls will also be given the opportunity to explore advertisements in common pre-adolescent and adolescent girls' magazines. They will be encouraged to discuss the content of the magazines: dieting, beauty tips, how to "catch" a man, friendships, careers, school, etc. Girls will learn how to identify the purpose of images and words in print advertisements with the intention of making them more aware of the often hidden connotations behind many of the messages they receive on a daily basis.

Media Stereotypes

Session Four Outline

1. Discuss: What are stereotypes? Give some examples of stereotypes. Differentiate between stereotypes and discrimination. It is important to note that stereotypes are often based on some truth; however, it is unfair to apply an assumption to an entire group of people.

2. Video Discussion: Crash – One More Time

3. *Real or Reel* discussion – Appendix D

   a. Ask girls to think of TV shows that contain stereotypes

   b. Discuss:

      i.   What impact does mass media have on our attitudes and beliefs?

      ii. What three groups are most often stereotyped in comedy shows? Why do you think this is the case?

4. Minority Report

   a. Give each girl a *Real People* worksheet and have them complete it – Appendix E

   b. Ask for volunteers to give examples from each category

   c. Discuss:

      i.   Which category was the most difficult? Easiest?

      ii. How are different groups of people treated here?

      iii. Who is treated with the least respect? Most?

      iv. What group has the most privileges? Least?

      v. What can be done to promote respect?

5. Girls and Media

   a. Divide into groups of two or three

   b. Give each group printed ads or allow them to use the internet to search for ads with pictures of females

   c. Each group should look at the ads and discuss the meaning

   d. Each girl should record the following in her notebook

      i.   Name of advertiser and product/service

      ii.   Describe the image including the girl/woman

      iii.   Does the image have anything to do with the product?

      iv.   What is the message about the product? Females?

      v.   Is this an effective ad? Why or why not?

   e. Each group will explain their ad to the large group

   f. Discuss the use of stereotypes in these advertisements

6. Digital Me or Real Girls Collage– continue work

7. Closing

   a. Name one thing you learned about someone else

   b. Name one thing you learned about yourself

8. Facilitator's Reflection

   a. Use the two page ***Facilitator's Notes*** to guide your reflections on this session

   b. Use the rubric to assess each girl's level of participation

Media Resources

Video

Crash – One More Time (www.wingclips.com)

- Television director Cameron is pressured to shoot another take of a scene, so as to perpetuate racial stereotypes.
- Discuss: What are your thoughts about this video? Do you think this happens?

The Boy in the Striped Pajamas – Nice Jew (www.wingclips.com)

- Bruno and his sister receive misinformation from a tutor about Jewish people.
- Discuss: Are stereotypes about a group of people ever entirely true? Why would people want to perpetuate stereotypes about themselves or others?

Crash – Blind Fear (www.wingclips.com)

- Anthony and Peter discuss how the poor service they received at a restaurant was due to racial stereotypes.
- Discuss: What are your thoughts about this video? Is it possible to be racist against people of your own race? Is it possible to be sexist against other females?

Scripture

Genesis 1:27 – So God created man in his own image, in the image of God he created him; male and female he created them.

Proverbs 31:30 – Charm is deceptive and beauty is fleeting; but a woman who fears the Lord is to be praised.

Romans 12:2 – Do not conform any longer to the pattern of this world, but be transformed by the renewing of your mind. Then you will be able to test and approve what God's will is – His good, pleasing, and perfect will.

Galatians 3:28 – There is neither Jew nor Greek, free nor slave, male nor female, for you are all one in Christ Jesus.

Romans 8:17 - Now if we are children, then we are heirs—heirs of God and co-heirs with Christ, if indeed we share in his sufferings in order that we may also share in his glory.

Audio

"Work That" by Mary J. Blige

Internet

- www.media-awareness.ca/english/issues/stereotyping/ - media stereotypes and the impact on young people
- http://www.media-awareness.ca/english/issues/stereotyping/women_and_girls/ - Stereotypes of girls/women in the media

Facilitator's Notes

Session Four – Media Stereotypes

Did most group members do the homework activity? What will you do to encourage them to complete group homework in the future?

_____

_____

_____

_____

What sort of comments did your group make during the **Real or Reel** discussion? Which shows were watched? Were you surprised by any of their comments?

_____

_____

_____

_____

What sort of comments did your group make during the video discussion? What ideas do you have for future discussion questions?

_____

_____

_____

_____

What sort of comments did your group make during the **Real People** discussion? What ideas do you have for other stereotypical categories to include in future discussions?

_____

_____

_____

_____

What sort of advertisements did your group find during the **Girls and Media** activity? What ideas do you have for using this activity in the future?

_____

_____

_____

_____

Is there anything you will do differently overall the next time you teach this specific session?

_____

_____

_____

_____

Additional thoughts:

_____

_____

_____

_____

Real Talk

Session Five

This session is focused on the ***power of positive thinking, including affirmations and self-talk***. Many girls spend valuable mental energy worrying about their weight, appearance, and clothing. They constantly tell themselves that they are not as good as their media idols. Repeatedly comparing themselves to the impossible ideals of fashion models and movie stars is discouraging for most girls, leading to more instances of low self-esteem, depression, and eating disorders.

During this session girls will learn how to identify negative thoughts and turn them into positive, realistic statements. They will work with a partner to role-play how to stop the cycle of negative self-talk that leads to low self-esteem and depression.

Next, girls will learn how to communicate their wants and needs in an ***assertive*** manner. This type of communication is ***focused on honest, respectful dialogue***. Assertive communication will be contrasted with aggressive and passive communication styles. Aggressive communication is hurtful to others. Girls sometimes say things that are considered mean or rude in an unsuccessful attempt to tell others how they feel. Girls may also engage in passive aggressive acts where they gossip or spread rumors about others in an attempt to get revenge for some perceived wrong that was done to them. Passive communication is typically done in a way that den es the needs or wants of that person. For instance, a girl is hurt because her friend does not invite her to the sleep over. If she were engaging in passive communication she may not say anything or may downplay her feelings of being hurt and excluded. Aggressive and passive communication styles do not result in helping girls build healthy relationships or positive self-concept.

To further the topic of communication, girls will be asked to respond to several "real situations." They will role-play how to hands common problems. Practicing an appropriate response is helpful in encouraging girls to think about their words and actions when difficult situations arise.

Girls will also discuss the importance of a positive attitude. It is commonly accepted that your attitude is the easiest thing in life to control; however, many adolescents allow their attitudes to be controlled by external circumstances. It is important for girls to know that they are able to **choose their response to any situation**. They may not be able to control what happens in every situation, but they can choose what they think about it.

With these topics girls will learn the importance of the words they speak to themselves and to others. They will also learn about the impact of their attitude on themselves and others.

Real Talk

Session Five Outline

1. Video Discussion: Gifted Hands – You Can Do This

2. Affirmations and Negative Self-Talk Intro

    a. Discuss the impact of self-talk

3. Stop the Negativity

    a. Divide into groups of two or three

    b. Each girl should say something negative she has thought about herself in the last week

    c. After this negative comment the partner will tell her to STOP

    d. Next, the first girl will change the negative comment into something more positive

    e. After each person has a turn, discuss with the group

4. Communication Role Play

    a. Create **Real Conversations** cards – Appendix F

    b. Explain aggressive, passive, and assertive communication

        i. Aggressive: expressing feelings in a way that violates the rights of others

        ii. Passive: failure to express needs, opinions, wants

        iii. Assertive: communicating what you want in a clear, respectful manner

    c. Ask for three volunteers to role play **Real Conversations** three times: first aggressive, next passive, then assertive

    d. Discuss:

        i. What pros and cons are there to each type?

  ii. Why is it sometimes more difficult to be assertive with people we care about the most?

5. Video Discussion: Saving God – 10 Seconds or Why Did I Get Married? – Don't Tempt Me

6. What Would You Do?

 a. Create a set of **Real Situations** cards – Appendix G

 b. Have a girl draw a card and say what she would do

 c. After a few volunteers have responded, ask the girls to create their own scenarios and discuss what they would do.

7. Digital Me or Real Girls Collage– continue work

8. Closing

 a. Discuss **Attitude** handout – Appendix H

 b. Name one thing you learned about someone else

 c. Name one thing you learned about yourself

9. Facilitator's Reflection

 a. Use the two page **Facilitator's Notes** to guide your reflections on this session

 b. Use the rubric to assess each girl's level of participation

Media Resources

Video

Gifted Hands – You Can Do This (www.wingclips.com)

- When her adult son begins to doubt his ability to perform a complex procedure, she encourages him that he can accomplish anything he sets his mind to.
- Discuss: Who in your life encourages you? What does she mean by "you've just gotta see beyond what you can see?"

Saving God – 10 Seconds (www.wingclips.com)

- Pastor Cain tells Norris the story of how a ten second mistake cost him 15 years in prison.
- Discuss: Do you know anyone who has made a mistake that still hurts them today? How does this video relate to communication? What could he have done to avoid going to prison?

An Angel for May – Not Possible (www.wingclips.com)

- Tom regrets saying some hurtful things to his mom and realizes that he can't go back and change it.
- Discuss: Have you ever said something you wish you could take back? What can you do to make positive decisions moving forward?

Scripture

Deuteronomy 11:18-19 – Fix these words of mine in your hearts and minds; tie them as symbols on your hands and bind them on your foreheads. Teach them to your children, talking about them when you sit at home and when you walk along the road, when you lie down and when you get up.

Proverbs 18:21 – The tongue has the power of life and death, and those who love it will eat its fruit.

Philippians 4:8 – Finally, brothers, whatever is true, whatever is noble, whatever is right, whatever is pure, whatever is lovely, whatever is admirable—if anything is excellent or praiseworthy—think about such things.

2 Corinthians 10:5 - We demolish arguments and every pretension that sets itself up against the knowledge of God, and we take captive every thought to make it obedient to Christ

Audio

"Six Feet Tall" by Never Say Never
"The Climb" by Miley Cyrus

Internet

- www.girlshealth.gov – Information about bullying, relationships, and feelings

Facilitator's Notes

Session Five – Real Talk

What sort of comments did your group make during the video discussion? What ideas do you have for future discussion questions?

_____

_____

_____

_____

How did your group respond to the role play activities? Did some group members participate more than others? What ideas do you have for future role plays activities?

_____

_____

_____

_____

What sort of comments did your group make during the second video discussion? What ideas do you have for future discussion questions?

_____

_____

_____

_____

_____

What sort of questions or concerns does your group have about the final group project? How much progress has been made? How can you help them finish on time?

_____

_____

_____

_____

How did your group respond to the **Attitude** handout discussion? Can you think of any other positive quotes to use in the future?

_____

_____

_____

_____

Is there anything you will do differently the next time you teach this specific session?

_____

_____

_____

_____

Additional thoughts:

_____

_____

_____

_____

_____

_____

Real Power

Session Six

> *God, grant me the serenity*
> *To accept the things I cannot change;*
> *Courage to change the things I can;*
> *And wisdom to know the difference.*
>
> > *-Reinhold Niebuhr*

While the previous session focused on communication and attitude, this session will focus on identifying what is within our control and what is not. Girls will learn to control those things they can and manage those things that are outside of their control.

Many girls spend a great deal of time worrying about things they cannot control, such as parents, teachers, and rules. The first activity in this session is designed to assist girls in identifying which of several topics they can control. They are instructed to place these things inside a circle. The other things, those they cannot control, are placed outside the circle. Girls are encouraged to focus more energy on controlling the things inside the circle.

Adolescents who choose to remain abstinent and substance free will need to learn to identify their limits and express those in an assertive manner. The next activity focuses on refusal skills. Girls will learn how to say "no" to things they do not want, while maintaining positive friendships.

Current research indicates that the most effective primary prevention programs for reducing marijuana and alcohol use among adolescents aged 10–15 years in the long-term were comprehensive programs that included information combined with refusal skills, self-management skills and social-skills training (Lemstra, Bennett, Nannapaneni, Newdorf, Warren, Kershaw, & Scott, 2010). The refusal skill activity is designed to support girls in their efforts to make positive decisions.

Refusal skills involve knowing how you feel ahead of time, being honest, and speaking only for yourself. Girls will discuss various ways of ***honestly expressing their limits and the consequences of going further***. Positive friendships can be maintained if girls learn to separate the person from the situation and suggest fun alternatives. Knowing how to state your decision and stick to it, without blaming anyone else, is a powerful way to resist peer pressure.

This session also includes discussion about peer pressure and how to avoid difficult situations, when needed. Girls will be encouraged to know what they want and leave situations that are not conducive to their goals.

Real Power

Session Six Outline

1. Video Discussion: When Zachary Beaver Came to Town

2. In The Box

    a. Draw a box. Ask girls which attributes it takes to fit in

    b. Draw a box. Ask girls to think of attributes of a good friend

    c. Discuss the differences

3. Where is the control?

    a. Create **Real Control** cards with things that girls may or may not have control over – Appendix I

    b. Draw a circle on the floor

    c. Pass out the cards to each girl and ask them to consider whether or not they control that thing

    d. Each girl should place her cards either inside (she controls it) or outside (not in her control) the circle to show where the control is located

    e. Discuss: Why is it important to know what you can and cannot control?

4. Power to Say No

    a. Give each girl a **Power to Say No** worksheet – Appendix J

    b. Provide a hypothetical difficult situation or ask girls to state a difficult situation

    c. Ask each girl to fill out the worksheet by writing statements that could be made for each section

    d. Ask volunteers to share their solutions to the situation

e. Discuss: Why is it important to practice refusal skills?

5. Digital Me or Real Girls Collage – continue work

6. Closing

    a. Name one thing you learned about someone else

    b. Name one thing you learned about yourself

7. Facilitator's Reflection

    a. Use the two page **Facilitator's Notes** to guide your reflections on this session

    b. Use the rubric to assess each girl's level of participation

Media Resources

Session Six – Real Power

Video

The Great Debaters – Righteous Mind (www.wingclips.com)

- Melvin educates his students about a slave owner's method of controlling his slaves. His strategy was to "keep the slave physically strong but psychologically weak and dependent on the slave owner."

- Discuss: What do you think about this video? How does this relate to the topic of sexual harassment? What impact does sexual harassment have on girls?

When Zachary Beaver Came to Town – I Dare You

(www.wingclips.com)

- Toby takes Cody up on a dare to climb the water tower and ends up in some real trouble.

- Discuss: What could he have done or said to avoid getting himself in that situation? Do your friends ever talk you into things that get you in trouble? How can you do what is right and keep your friends?

Scripture

Philippians 4:13 – I can do everything through Him who gives me strength.

2 Corinthians 12:20 – That is why, for Christ's sake, I delight in weaknesses, in insults, in hardships, in persecutions, in difficulties. For when I am weak, then I am strong.

Proverbs 24:5-6 – A wise man has great power, and a man of knowledge increases strength; for waging war you need guidance, and for victory many advisers

Ephesians 3:20 – Now to him who is able to do immeasurably more than all we ask or imagine, according to his power that is at work within us

Audio

"Fighter" by Christina Aguilera

"Respect" by Aretha Franklin

Internet

- www.wingclips.com – Movie clips organized by topic
- http://family.samhsa.gov/teach/refusal.aspx - How to teach youth to say "no"
- http://mychoice2wait.org/refusal.html - Abstinence-based refusal skills

Facilitator's Notes

Session Six – Real Power

What sort of comments did your group make during the video discussion? What ideas do you have for future discussion questions?

_____

_____

_____

_____

How did your group respond to the opening activity? Were there any surprises as to what makes a person popular? What ideas do you have for future opening activities?

_____

_____

_____

_____

What sort of comments did your group make during the **Real Control** discussion? What ideas do you have for topics to include in the future?

_____

_____

_____

_____

_____

What sort of comments did your group make during the **Power to Say No** discussion? What ideas do you have for future discussion questions?

_____

_____

_____

_____

What concerns do you have about the group process? How will you resolve these concerns?

_____

_____

_____

_____

Is there anything you will do differently the next time you teach this specific session?

_____

_____

_____

_____

Additional thoughts:

_____

_____

_____

_____

_____

_____

Healthy Relationships

Session Seven

In order for young girls to develop healthy relationships it is important for them to recognize key components of what constitutes a healthy relationship. Healthy relationships are relationships that promote positive interactions, appropriate boundaries, enhance the quality of both parties and challenge each party to grow and become a better person. According to the Medical Institute for Sexual Health (2005), healthy relationships are "ones in which there's a strong foundation of similarities in background, temperament, goals, dreams, values, and the way in which individuals managed and ordered their physical and mental lives."

Relationships that promote positive interactions are relationships, in which both parties are valued and respected as unique individuals; each party having something special to offer the other. Healthy relationships are built around supportive behavior patterns, which value the opinions of each party and respect the differences of each party. Understanding the core principles of positive interactions in relationships may assist young girls in choosing more positive friendships.

Appropriate boundaries are critical in the development of healthy relationships. Clearly defining boundaries for young girls and what they look like in a healthy relationship is vital for the development of positive peer relationships. This is vital because relationships where appropriate boundaries are not valued may lead to physical and or emotional abuse. According to a recent report, one in four youth ages 11-14 says dating violence (physically hurting relationship partners) is a serious problem for people their age (Liz Claiborne, Inc/Teen Research Unlim ted, 2008). Several adolescents experience not only physical abuse, but also emotional abuse in peer relationships. Unfortunately, the statistics reveal that the number of unhealthy relationships increases with age. These statistics are alarming and illustrate the need for young girls to be better educated on the importance of appropriate boundaries, when engaging in a relationship.

The activities in this session will focus on healthy versus unhealthy relationships. Girls will discuss various types of healthy and unhealthy relationships. They will learn key components of healthy relationships (respect, communication and boundaries) and warning signs of potentially unhealthy relationships (jealously, control, physical and verbal abuse).

Healthy Relationships

Session Seven Outline

1. Video Discussion: Choose Respect video (13 mins)

    a. http://www.cdc.gov/chooserespect/materials_and_resources /causing_pain_video_discussion.html

    b. Pause the video every 2-3 minutes to engage in discussion about the message

2. Discuss: What is a healthy relationship? What observable behaviors define a healthy relationship? Why is it important to know what a healthy relationship looks like? How does the media portray relationships?

3. Video Discussion: Diary of A Mad Black Woman – either

    a. Discuss: How can jealousy be mistaken for love? Why do some people think jealousy is a normal part of a relationship?

    b. Explain that jealousy is a normal emotion, but what you do with it is what determines whether or not it is abusive or controlling

4. Boundaries

    a. Divide girls into groups of 3 or 4

    b. Give each group a set of ***Boundary-Crossing Behavior*** cards and a set of ***Boundary-Crossing Categories*** cards – Appendix K

    c. Explain the following:

      i.   *Unwelcome sexual advances*: suggesting sexual activity with a person by constantly calling, text messaging, or visiting with them

     ii.   *Requests for sexual favors*: asking a person for sexual activity in return for a promotion, grade, money, or some other reward

   iii.   *Verbal conduct of a sexual nature*: unwanted sexual comments, jokes, notes, rumors, etc.

   iv.   *Physical conduct of a sexual nature*: inappropriate and unwanted touching

d. Ask each group to place the four **Boundary-Crossing Category** cards face up on the table, then pick up one **Boundary-Crossing Behavior** card at a time and put it in the right category

e. Discuss: The law is concerned with the "impact not the intent" of the behavior. What does that mean? How can sexual harassment hinder a person in the workplace? In school?

5. Digital Me or Real Girls Collage – continue work

6. Closing

a. Name one thing you learned about someone else

b. Name one thing you learned about yourself

7. Facilitator's Reflection

a. Use the two page **Facilitator's Notes** to guide your reflections on this session

b. Use the rubric to assess each girl's level of participation

Media Resources

Video

Diary of A Mad Black Woman – Get Even (www.wingclips.com)

- After being shot and crippled, Charles was deserted by his new family and friends with no one to care for him but his ex-wife Helen, who he had spent years abusing and abandoned.

- Discuss: What do you think about this video? Who has the power in this video clip? What types of abuse do you see in this video?

Diary of A Mad Black Woman – Don't Be Like Me (www.wingclips.com)

- As payback for years of abuse, Helen has been mistreating her now-crippled ex-husband. Realizing the extent of the hurt he caused her, Charles urges her not to be like him.

- Discuss: Why do you think about this video? Was it right for Helen to mistreat Charles?

Scripture

2 Corinthians 6:14 – Do not be yoked together with unbelievers. For what do righteousness and wickedness have in common? Or what fellowship can light have with darkness?

2 Corinthians 6:18 – I will be a Father to you, and you will be my sons and daughters, says the Lord Almighty.

Psalm 5:11 – But let all who take refuge in you be glad; let them ever sing for joy. Spread your protection over them, that those who love your name may rejoice in you.

John 17:15 – My prayer is not that you take them out of the world but that you protect them from the evil one.

Audio

"Fighter" by Christina Aguilera

"Respect" by Aretha Franklin

"Lessons Learned" by Carrie Underwood

Internet

- www.wingclips.com – Movie clips organized by topic
- www.loveisrespect.org – Teen dating abuse information

Facilitator's Notes

Session Seven – Healthy Relationships

What sort of comments did your group make during the video discussion? What ideas do you have for future discussion questions?

_____

_____

_____

_____

How did your group respond to the discussion about healthy relationships? What difficulty did you have discussing these sensitive topics?

_____

_____

_____

_____

How did your group respond to the **_Boundaries_** discussion? What difficulty did you have discussing these sensitive topics?

_____

_____

_____

_____

_____

What sort of questions or concerns does your group have about the final group project? How much progress has been made? How can you help them finish on time?

_____

_____

_____

_____

What concerns do you have about the group process? How will you resolve these concerns?

_____

_____

_____

_____

Is there anything you will do differently the next time you teach this specific session?

_____

_____

_____

_____

Additional thoughts:

_____

_____

_____

_____

_____

_____

Digital Me/Collage

Session Eight

This session is focused on the final stage in the group process: adjourning. Girls have worked hard over the past seven sessions. They have discussed sensitive material, formed close friendships, and created lasting bonds. This is their time to complete any outstanding tasks and celebrate what they have done. Girls will also complete a post-group survey, found at the end of this book.

Each girl should have created a digital story about her life. This digital story will be shared with the entire group. Girls will have the opportunity to think about any difficulties they had in telling their story. They will also engage in discussion about how others' stories impacted them.

This project was chosen because of the great need for adolescents to practice self-reflection. ***When girls are able to think about their previous actions, they are able to make better choices in the future.*** Unfortunately, many youth progress from day-to-day and month-to-month without reflecting on how their actions impact their future. This type of activity will assist girls in beginning to think about the fact that actions have long-term consequences.

Each girl will handle this separation in a different way. Some girls will be excited to use what they have learned in their daily lives. They may also be happy about completing something important. Some girls will need encouragement to think about how they can continue to grow using the self-reflection techniques and critical thinking skills they have learned.

Some girls may experience sadness or anxiety at the end of the group. It is important to be sensitive to these emotions as they arise in individual girls. ***They should be encouraged to think of ways to extend the experience of girl community beyond the end of this group.*** There are several existing national organizations that focus on girl development: Girl Scouts, Girls Inc., and Girls on The Run. Additional nonprofit organizations may exist in your community, including church youth groups, after school programs, and recreational sports.

As the group facilitator, you have used the ***Facilitator's Notes*** pages to reflect on each session. After this final group you are encouraged to think about the entire program. There will be activities that you and your girls loved; however, there will also be activities that did not appeal to your group. It is important to think about how you will modify the activities in the future to make them more relevant to your girls. It may be wise to keep a list of the songs, movies, and magazines that your girls referenced during the sessions. These could be used in future groups to make the material more engaging.

Remember to thank the girls for their hard work, congratulate them on completing the program, and encourage them to support one another as they continue to grow.

Digital Me/Collage

Session Eight Outline

1. Wrap-up

   a. Thank the girls for participating

   b. Have each girl complete a post-survey

2. Share each Real Girls project

   a. Have each girl share their Real Girls project

   b. Discuss:

       i.   What did you learn from completing this project?

       ii.   What part of the project was the most difficult? Easiest?

       iii. What will you do with what you have learned from this project?

3. Refreshments and Celebration

4. Facilitator's Reflection

   a. Use the two page ***Facilitator's Notes*** to guide your reflections on this session

   b. Spend some time reflecting on the entire group process, with a focus on what you may do differently in the future

   c. Use the rubric to assess each girl's level of participation

Media Resources

Session Eight – Digital Me/Collage

Video

I Can Do Bad All By Myself – Smile (www.wingclips.com)

- Madea urges the young and depressed Jennifer to smile more often and appreciate the attributes that she has been blessed with.
- Discuss: What do you think about this video? What is Madea asking Jennifer to do about her attitude?

Bella – A Beautiful Day (www.wingclips.com)

- A blind man asks to exchange a gift for Nina's description of the New York scenery.
- Discuss: Why do you think about this video?

Scripture

2 Corinthians 13:11 – Finally, brothers, goodbye. Aim for perfection, listen to my appeal, be of one mind, live in peace. And the God of love and peace will be with you.

Audio

"Fighter" by Christina Aguilera

"Respect" by Aretha Franklin

"Lessons Learned" by Carrie Underwood

Facilitator's Notes

Session Eight – Real Girls

How did your group develop during the course of this eight session discussion? Are there any areas of unexpected growth?

_____

_____

_____

_____

In which areas (self-concept, media awareness, and/or healthy relationships) would you like to see more growth? What can you do differently in the future?

_____

_____

_____

_____

Overall, how did your group respond to the video discussions? What ideas do you have for future video clips or discussion questions?

_____

_____

_____

_____

Overall, how did your group respond to the role-play activities? What ideas do you have for future engaging, cooperative activities?

_____

_____

_____

_____

What concerns do you have about the group process? How will you resolve these concerns the next time you work with a group?

_____

_____

_____

_____

How did your group respond to the Real Girls project? What insights did you gain from their work?

_____

_____

_____

_____

Additional thoughts:

_____

_____

_____

_____

_____

_____

Media Analysis Guide

*It is the work of true education to develop this
power, to train young people to be thinkers, and not
mere reflectors of other people's thoughts.*
                    -Delyse Steyn

The purpose of this section is to describe how to use any media source
in discussing topics related to self-concept, media awareness, and
healthy relationships. We will cover the definition of media literacy, how
to collect media samples, several techniques of media analysis, and the
rights of media consumers.

Media Literacy

Literacy is traditionally thought of as the ability to read and write text.
The skills associated with literacy allow us to use written messages to
communicate with others, understand information, and participate in
the world. Twentieth century technology requires us to expand the
concept of literacy from text to all visual and printed media.

Media literacy is commonly understood to be a set of tools that
assist a person in interpreting, analyzing, and creating messages
received through various media formats. The primary goal of media
literacy education is to teach people how to be mindful, rather than
mindless, when consuming media messages.

Collecting Media Samples

Using engaging, relevant media samples is important to the success of any media literacy discussion. You will want to search magazines, movies, commercials, television shows, songs, and Internet websites for images and videos that address a range of topics. Please consult the resources at the end of this book for suggested books, videos, and websites. While these resources will allow you to obtain current information, girls are usually happy to share their favorite music artists, actresses, and shows.

These media messages will need to be organized by topic for easy access and use. A few of the topics explored in this book include body image, relationships, sexuality, and substance use. It may be wise to begin saving digital copies of all media messages into folders, labeled with your topics of interest. These folders can be further divided by type of media.

Media Analysis Techniques

Media analysis consists of a set of tools or skills that can be applied to various media formats. The techniques include knowing foundational information that applies to all media: media content is created for a specific audience, with a specific purpose. A basic understanding of advertising techniques will also help girls deconstruct media messages (Media Literacy Project, 2010). Based on this information, facilitators can begin to ask questions about the media sample. The questions on the next page were adapted from the MediaLit Kit (Center for Media Literacy, 2008).

Center for Media Literacy: Key Questions

- Who created the message? What technology was used? What choices were made that could have been different?
- What techniques were used to attract attention? What do you see first? Are there any visual symbols? What is the emotional appeal?
- How might different people understand this message differently? How close is this message to reality? What other viewpoints are missing?
- What values, lifestyles, and points of view are represented in, or omitted from, this message? What values are being sold? What is the overall worldview? What is the person's character?
- Why is this message being created? Who profits or benefits from the message? Who are they sending the message to? Why are they sending the message? What economic decisions influenced the message construction and/or transmission?

Advertising Techniques

- Humor: Laugh, be happy, buy this product.
- Bandwagon: Everyone is doing it, you should too.
- Sexy or famous people: You can be like these sexy or famous people if you buy this product.
- Linking: If you like this product, you should like this other product or activity too. (often seen with alcohol/sexuality and teens)
- Be cool: If you buy this you will be popular.
- Sexuality: Sexual images are used to sell everything.

Rights of Consumers

It is important to know your rights in all areas of life in order to fully participate in society. As media consumers, youth and adults have many basic rights. If these rights were realized and utilized the media may not have such a negative impact on today's girls.

Youth have the right to choose what they watch. They do not have to watch shows that consistently portray negative stereotypes. Girls, in particular, can choose to purchase magazines with positive articles about relationships, school, and health, rather than typical fashion magazines with articles about attracting boys, losing weight, and wearing sexy clothing.

Girls also have the right to speak up about what they think of current media creation, including advertising (Howard, 2009). They can write letters to producers and editors to express their views. Emails and phone calls can also be a powerful way to demonstrate that a new form of marketing is needed.

Parents have the right to limit their child's viewing of certain media sources; however, censorship has been shown to backfire. Youth can access their desired media in many different locations, including friends' homes, grocery stores, and school. An alternative for parents is to use their right to discuss media with their children. This gives youth the tools to be conscious consumers.

Finally, girls have the right to create their own media messages. Several girls have created web-based magazines, girl-edited books, and positive social marketing that are reaching girls across the nation.

Parent Guide

If a child or teenager does not feel the warmth of love, no other tactic is going to work.

-Ross Wright

The *Real Girls* guide can be a great starting point for parents who want to communicate more effectively with their daughters. Several research studies clearly state that youth do better on many levels (socially, emotionally, and academically) when their parents are actively engaged in their lives (Adolescent Substance Abuse Knowledge Base, 2007; Centers for Disease Control, 2006; Kaiser Family Foundation, 2010). Youth who have open communication with their parents struggle less with issues of low self-esteem and are also less likely to engage in destructive behaviors. Building a healthy relationship with your child is critical for their future success. Current research indicates that "*all children need relationships in order to fill up the areas of character and self identity inside them*" (The Medical Institute for Sexual Health, 2005). Utilizing this guide will provide you with a fun, interactive, and engaging way to spend time with your daughter(s), while promoting their positive self-image.

Outlined below are communication tips that may assist you in using the *Real Girls* curriculum with your child. These tips are taken from the Child Welfare League of America (n.d.).

- Kids deserve respect, and adults should give it to them and expect it from them. Think about how often you ask teenagers questions and seek their opinions.

- Teens are apprentice adults, and they need room to breathe and learn the trade. It's up to the adult to balance freedom and independence with good judgment about when to step in.
- Make a point to talk with teens when there is no problem.
- Make sure you listen carefully to what is being said, as well as what is not.

This section offers practical steps to engage in open dialogue with your child, while using the *Real Girls* curriculum. When communicating with your daughter try to ask open-ended questions rather than close-ended questions. Open-ended questions are questions that allow room for varied responses. An example of an open-ended question would be: *Tell me about your day at school.* As opposed to a close-ended question: *How was your day at school?* The difference in the two may appear insignificant, however the impact is monumental. We will explore this further: asking your daughter to tell you about her day at school will allow her to discuss any and everything, whether it was positive or negative. This will provide an opportunity for flexibility in the conversation, which can improve the quality of the overall discussion between you and your child. Asking your daughter, "how was your day at school" may leave you with a more restricted response, such as o.k., good, not bad. After gaining a narrow response like this it may be difficult to illicit more detailed information, as your daughter may now feel that you are being "nosey."

Remaining neutral during your conversation with your daughter is critical. It is important to know that when youth feel like they are being judged they are less likely to share openly with adults. Although it may not be a topic of conversation you enjoy, validating your child and affirming them without displaying judgment will make them feel more respected, which may make it easier for them to communicate with you. As a parent this may be a difficult and uncomfortable process initially; however, once the tone has be set, you may find that this becomes more natural. Remaining neutral does not mean that you do not take an active parenting role and clearly provide rules and boundaries for your child because after all, that is what parenting is all about.

When using the *Real Girls* curriculum with your daughter you can modify each session according to the resources you currently have available to you. You may also decide to add interesting video clips, magazine ads, or TV programs to the recommended materials. A great resource that may assist you in obtaining added materials is DiscoverYourDaughter.com and Discovery Girls Magazine. This process can be enjoyable for both you and your daughter, as it allows more time for communication and engagement. This can be an opportunity for growth for each of you; it can also provide your daughter with a deeper understanding of your viewpoints and perspective concerning media, technology, and other social outlets.

Church Youth Group Guide

Cinema is a modern day pulpit. Movie theaters are not so different from church assemblies; people flock to their local multiplexes, group together, and find themselves moved by a worldview revealed in story form, allowing themselves to be emotionally led by directors and screenwriters who influence how we feel, think, and even act.

- James Harleman, Founder of Cinemagogue

Real Girls can be a great resource for church youth groups, who work primarily with middle and high school age girls. Each session in *Real Girls* has biblical Christian scriptures aligned with the purpose of the lesson. This allows youth to see God's influence in their daily lives as it relates to media, relationships, and their identity development. Making things relevant to youth is critical to their engagement and success in any group and/or program. When youth feel like they are connected to something that is beneficial to them, the likelihood of their participation and completion is much higher.

As a church youth group leader, *Real Girls* can be implemented in a practical and engaging way by allowing the youth to make connections with current bible lessons and the sessions outlined in *Real Girls.* An example of this would be reviewing session 7, Healthy Relationships, and making a connection between Sampson and Delilah in the bible. This would make room for a very dynamic discussion and lesson about the importance of choices, when choosing your friends. In the bible, Sampson chose a woman who God did not choose for him and his God given power was lost. Again, not only are you sharing God's truth, but you are also making it relevant to the youth in today's time. You can utilize each session in *Real Girls* in this type of format because the sessions are very practical. Each session illustrates the different struggles that young girls currently experience.

Another very practical way that youth church leaders can utilize the program is to add Christian media (magazines, movies, websites, songs, etc.) to each session and have youth compare the Christian media to the media resources listed in *Real Girls.* This may provide a unique opportunity for youth to see how culture is shaped by several perspectives and ideologies. Youth may also gain knowledge of the importance of sharing God's truth with others, so that others can be shaped by truth and not solely by what is shown to them through social media.

James McDonnell (1992) believes that "following Christ in a media culture demands that we become aware of how we use the media and how much we depend on the media to shape the routine of our lives." Youth, as well as adults, need to know that our ultimate guidance comes from the Lord, not from social media. It is important to remember that the purpose of media creation is to make money, at any cost.

Biblical principles can be applied to any media (television, movies, music, Internet, video games, magazines, etc.) by comparing them to the over-arching story of creation, the fall, salvation, and the new creation. According to Bruce Ashford (2010), there are nine elements in movies that can be analyzed in light of the bible. Using the questions in the following table will allow youth to understand that there is a bigger story behind the flashing lights and loud music. After asking and answering the questions, youth will be able to discern whether they want to identify with the characters and how their values line up with those shown in the media.

Nine Elements

Element	What it Shows	Questions to Ask
Theme	The message, ultimate point	Does this theme resonate with what I know to be true and good?
Hero	Main character	Does the hero correct his character flaws? How? Is he/she virtuous? Does he/she stand for what is true and good?
Hero's goal	Strong desire, drives the movie	Is the hero's goal admirable? Are there any ways it is wrong or misguided?
Adversary	Opposes the hero: person, animal, force, God	Is the adversary actually bad? Is it something I actually disagree with?
Character flaw	Internal opponent: action, worldview	Is it really a flaw? Does he/she rely on God's grace to correct it? Does he/she acknowledge the flaw?
Apparent defeat	Thwarted by his flaw and adversary	Whose strength is he/she relying on to overcome the opponent?
Final confrontation	Worldviews in conflict	Should I oppose this adversary and his rationale?
Self-revelation	Aha moment of the hero	Is this self-revelation a good one?
Resolution	Result of the hero's decisions and actions	Is this a realistic result? It this a good result?

In addition to the questions in the previous table, John Frame (2005) proposes a series of questions that can be asked of movies, regarding the presence of Christian ideals, Christ-figures, religious themes, and allusions to history. The answers to these questions can be the basis for discussion around topics of significance to youth who are searching for their true identity.

When identity development is approached from a Christian worldview it is possible to move beyond the fluctuations of day-to-day life for the typical young girl. Adolescents who claim to rely on religious beliefs in uncertain situations are more likely to refuse alcoholic drinks, turn to religious leaders for advice, and refrain from having sex before marriage (Girl Scout Research Institute, 2009). Unfortunately, the percentage of girls surveyed who reported being religious was below 20%.

As the authors, we believe that girls across the country have a voice that is waiting to be heard. However, it is difficult for many young girls to speak up when they are faced with issues of low self-concept, the bombardment of negative media influences, the cycle of unhealthy relationships and the identity struggles that they are faced with. During the journey from youth to womanhood, the voices of many young girls often become mere echoes as they attempt to navigate their way in life. It is our hope that *Real Girls* can be a tool used to aide young girls in freeing their voice, which may empower them to then free the voices of other young girls, who may face similar struggles. We hope that this book encourages you, the reader, as you continue to uplift young girls and empower them to be the "real girls" that they are.

"Through media education and literacy, the creation of media subcultures, participation in athletics, comprehensive sex education programs, activism, and religious/spiritual practices, girls, their peers, adults in their lives, and institutions that support them help to challenge the narrow prescriptions for girls in this culture."

(American Psychological Association, Task Force on the Sexualization of Girls, 2007, p. 36)

Movie Clips

Knowing Yourself

Dead Poets Society (PG) — **Studio:** Touchstone, **Directed by:** Peter Weir

Plot: An unorthodox English teacher in a private prep school both challenges and inspires his young students to think for themselves and live life to the fullest. His motto for them is simple, yet life-changing: Carpe diem, or "Seize the day!"

Theme: Independent Thinking

Discussion Questions: What is your special walk? Why do we find ourselves conforming to others? How important is it to fit in with the crowd? What do we think of someone who chooses not to participate at all?

Back to the Future (PG) — **Studio:** Universal, **Directed by:** Robert Zemekis

Plot: Marty McFly gets shot back in time to the days when his parents were in high school. In the local soda shop where the future mayor sweeps up, Marty meets the teenage version of his dad, who is about to have one of many run-ins with the local bully.

Theme: Standing Up to Power

Discussion Questions: How could George stand up for himself? Why is it hard sometimes to stand up to others? What holds us back?

A Walk to Remember (PG) – Studio: Warner Brothers,

Directed by: Karen Janszen

Plot: Based on the novel by Nicholas Sparks, this is the story of a girl firmly grounded in her religious beliefs who finds herself attracted to a boy whose life and background are quite the opposite of hers.

Theme: Who Are Your Friends

Discussion Questions: Does it matter what people think about you? Why? Why not? What does it mean to be self-confident? Whose opinions do matter to you? How many people really know you?

Notes/thoughts: _____

_____

_____

_____

_____

_____

_____

_____

_____

Facing Peer Pressure

Drumline (PG-13) - **Theme:** Responsibility for Others
Studio: 20th Century Fox, **Directed by:** Charles Stone III
Plot: A kid from Harlem is recruited into a southern university marching band. Thinking that he is the answer to all the band's problems does not score him any points with the tough band professor. Everyone needs a lesson in what it means to work as a team, and what it means to be responsible for one another.
Discussion Questions: What is the difference between helpful and harmful peer pressure? Are we responsible for other's actions? Why or why not?

Sky High (G) - **Theme:** Using Popularity as a Weapon
Studio: Walt Disney, **Directed by:** Mike Mitchell
Plot: It is not easy to be the powerless son of the most famous superheroes on the planet. At least his best friend is always there for him. But when his powers finally emerge will there still be room in his new life for the friend he has left behind?
Discussion Questions: How do you know if someone is telling you the truth? What should you do when you hear something bad about a friend? What does it mean to be really loyal?

A Christmas Story (PG) - **Theme:** Standing Up to a Dare

Studio: MGM, **Directed by:** Bob Clark

Plot: This tale may be set in the 1940s, but the situations these kids face are very familiar today. For example, when a friend dares you to do something that you know is not a good idea, what will you choose to do?

Discussion Questions: Do crowds influence what we say and do? How? Why? What makes a dare so powerful? What would happen if we said "no" to a dare?

Mean Girls (PG-13) - **Theme:** Cliques as Bullies

Studio: Paramount, **Directed by:** Mark Waters

Plot: When a girl who has always been home-schooled suddenly enters a public high school, she learns that it can be pretty hard to fit in. So, when some popular girls invite her to join their clique, it seems like a great idea...or is it?

Discussion Questions: What are the rules your friends expect you to follow? What is a clique? How can a clique be harmful? How can cliques control you?

Notes/thoughts: _____

_____

_____

_____

_____

_____

Self-Control

Jimmy Neutron — **Theme:** Self-Discipline

Studio: Paramount, **Directed by:** John A. Davis

Plot: Aliens abduct all adults; genius Jimmy and his friends build an interstellar spacefleet and rescue them.

Scene: The neighborhood kids go nuts when they learn all the parents are gone.

Discussion Questions: When is goofing around okay? When isn't it okay? What makes a "mature" person?

Sea Biscuit — **Theme:** Letting Go

Studio: Universal Pictures, **Directed by:** Gary Ross

Plot: True story of the undersized Depression-era racehorse whose victories lifted not only the spirits of the team behind it but also those of the nation as well.

Scene: Red gets upset when another jockey cuts him off during a race.

Discussion Questions: Why do people get angry? Some people say that we only get angry when we feel that we may partly be to blame for the problem. Do you agree or disagree? Do you ever feel "out of control" when you are angry? What are some ways you can manage your anger so that it works in everyone's best interest?

Finding Nemo – Theme: Avoiding/Facing Temptation

Studio: Pixar Animation, **Directed by**: Andrew Stanton & Lee Unkrich (co-director)

Plot: A father-son underwater adventure featuring Nemo, a boy clownfish, stolen from his coral reef home. His timid father must then travel to Sydney, and search Sydney Harbour find Nemo.

Scene: A shark tries to obstain from eating fish.

Discussion Questions: Do friends help you resist temptation or are they more often the source of temptation? How does peer pressure contribute to your ability to resist temptation? What personal qualities are necessary to resist doing the wrong thing?

Notes/thoughts: _____

_____

_____

_____

_____

_____

_____

_____

_____

_____

_____

_____

Honesty

<u>**Liar Liar**</u> – **Theme:** White Lies

Studio: Universal, **Directed by:** Tom Shadyac

Plot: A fast track lawyer can't lie for 24 hours due to his son's birthday wish after the lawyer turns his son down for the last time.

Scene: Fletcher tries to convince his on that white lies are okay.

Discussion Questions: With which character do you relate? Have you told a lie to save someone you know from being hurt by the truth?

<u>**Shrek**</u> – **Theme:** Hiding in Fear

Studio: Dreamworks Animation, **Directed by:** Andrew Adamson & Vicky Jenson

Plot: An ogre, in order to regain his swamp, travels along with an annoying donkey in order to bring a princess to a scheming lord, wishing himself King.

Scene: Princes Fiona explains why she can't tell the truth about herself.

Discussion Questions: Have you ever had something go wrong because you were afraid to tell the truth?

<u>Cool Runnings</u> – Theme: Winning At All Costs

Studio: Disney, **Directed by:** Jon Turteltaub

Plot: Based on the true story of the First Jamacian bobsled team trying to make it to the winter olympics.

Scene: Derice asks his coach why he cheated in the Olympics.

Discussion Questions: Are the successful people you know truthful people? Are they people who keep their promises?

Notes/thoughts: _____

_____

_____

_____

_____

_____

_____

_____

_____

_____

_____

_____

_____

_____

_____

_____

_____

_____

_____

_____

_____

Respect

Remember the Titans – **Theme:** Getting to Know You

Studio: Disney, **Directed by**: Boaz Yakin

Plot: The true story of a newly appointed African-American coach and his high school team on their first season as a racially integrated unit.

Scene: Coach Boone informs the team that thy will have to get to know one another.

Discussion Questions: What divisions do you see around you: black/white, in-crowd/out-crowd etc.? How can you overcome those divisions?

X-Men – **Theme:** Fitting In

Studio: Fox, **Directed by:** Bryan Singer

Plot: Two mutants come to a private academy for mutants whose resident superhero team must oppose a powerful mutant terrorist organization.

Scene: Professor Xavier explains why school is a haven for outcast mutants.

Discussion Questions: Have people ever looked down on you because of how you looked or acted? Have you treated someone badly because of how they looked or acted?

<u>Babe</u> – **Theme:** Earning the Right to Lead

Studio: Universal, **Directed by:** Chris Noonan

Plot: Babe, a pig raised by sheepdogs, learns to herd sheep with a little help from Farmer Hoggett.

Scene: Babe learns how far politness can get him.

Discussion Questions: When have you seen a person exemplify bad leadership? How easy is it to respect that person? How can they regain respect?

Notes/thoughts: _____

_____

_____

_____

_____

_____

_____

_____

_____

_____

_____

_____

_____

_____

_____

Music Lyrics

"Beautiful Flower" by India Aire

This is a song for every girl who's

Ever been through something

she thought she couldn't make it through

I sing these words because I was that girl too

Wanting something better than this, But who do I turn to

Now we're moving from the darkness into the light

This is the defining moment of our lives

'Cause you're beautiful like a flower,

More valuable than a diamond

You are powerful like a fire,

You can heal the world with your mind

(Chorus)

There is nothing in the world that you cannot do

When you believe in you, who are beautiful

Yeah, you, who are brilliant;

Yeah, you, who are powerful;

Yeah, you, who are resilient

This is a song for every girl who

Feels like she is not special

'Cause she don't look like a supermodel Coke bottle

The next time the radio tells you to

shake your moneymaker

Shake your head and tell them,

tell them you're a leader

Now we're moving from the darkness into the light

This is the defining moment of our lives

'Cause you're beautiful like a flower,

More valuable than a diamond

You are powerful like a fire,

You can heal the world with your mind

(Chorus)

Discuss:

- What do you think about hearing that you are beautiful, brilliant, powerful, and resilient?
- What does it mean to move from darkness into light?
- What do you think about the line that says "*The next time the radio tells you to shake your moneymaker, shake your head and tell them, tell them you're a leader*"?

Music Lyrics

"Just a Girl" by No Doubt

Take this pink ribbon off my eyes; I'm exposed

And it's no big surprise

Don't you think I know exactly where I stand

This world is forcing me to hold your hand

'Cause I'm just a girl, little ol' me;

Don't let me out of your sight

I'm just a girl, all pretty and petite,

so don't let me have any rights

Oh. . . I've had it up to here!

The moment that I step outside,

so many reasons for me to run and hide

I can't do the little things I hold so dear

'Cause it's all those little things that I fear

'Cause I'm just a girl, I'd rather not be

'Cause they won't let me drive late at night

I'm just a girl; Guess I'm some kind of freak

'Cause they all sit and stare with their eyes,

I'm just a girl;

Take a good look at me, just your typical prototype

Oh. . . I've had it up to here!

Oh. . . am I making myself clear?

I'm just a girl; I'm just a girl in the world. . .

That's all that you'll let me be!

I'm just a girl, living in captivity
Your rule of thumb makes me worry some
I'm just a girl, what's my destiny?
What I've succumbed to is making me numb
I'm just a girl, my apologies;
What I've become is so burdensome
I'm just a girl, lucky me;
Twiddle-dum there's no comparison

Oh. . . I've had it up to; Oh. . . I've had it up to;
Oh. . . I've had it up to here.

Discuss:

- What do you think about the role of girls in society?
- Why do you think she says she's "rather not be" a girl?
- Why do you think she says there are "so many reasons for [her] to run and hide"? What do you think girls need to hide from?
- Do you think there are different rules for girls than for boys?

Music Lyrics

*"**Beautiful**" by Christina Aguilera*

(Spoken) Don't look at me

Every day is so wonderful and suddenly, I saw debris

Now and then, I get insecure from all the pain,

I'm so ashamed

I am beautiful no matter what they say;

Words can't bring me down

I am beautiful in every single way;

Yes, words can't bring me down

So don't you bring me down today

To all your friends, you're delirious,

so consumed in all your doom

Trying hard to fill the emptiness;

The piece is gone left the puzzle undone

That's the way it is

You are beautiful no matter what they say;

Words can't bring you down

You are beautiful in every single way;

Yes, words can't bring you down

Don't you bring me down today...

No matter what we do; No matter what they say

When the sun is shining through,

then the clouds won't stay

And everywhere we go; The sun won't always shine

But tomorrow will find a way; All the other times

'cause we are beautiful no matter what they say

Yes, words won't bring us down, oh no

We are beautiful in every single way;

Yes, words can't bring us down

Don't you bring me down today

Don't you bring me down today;

Don't you bring me down today

Discuss:

- Do you believe that words have the power to bring you down?

- What does it mean to be insecure? What are some girls insecure about?

- Who do you think she is talking to when she says, "Don't you bring me down today?" Could she be talking to friends, family, media, or herself?

- What would it feel like to be beautiful "in every single way?"

Music Lyrics

"*Fighter*" by Christina Aguilera

When I, thought I knew you; Thinking, that you were true

I guess I, I couldn't trust, 'Cause your bluff time is up,

'Cause I've had enough

You were, there by my side; Always, down for the ride

But your, joy ride just came down in flames

'Cause your greed sold me out of shame, mmhmm

After all of the stealing and cheating

You probably think that I hold resentment for you

But, uh uh, oh no, you're wrong

'Cause if it wasn't for all that you tried to do

I wouldn't know just how capable I am to pull through

So I wanna say thank you

(Chorus)

'Cause it makes me that much stronger;

Makes me work a little bit harder

It makes me that much wiser;

So thanks for making me a fighter

Made me learn a little bit faster;

Made my skin a little bit thicker

Makes me that much smarter;

So thanks for making me a fighter...Ohhh

Never, saw it coming; All of, your backstabbing

Just so, you could cash in on a good thing

before I realized your game

I heard, you're going around playing, the victim now

But don't, even begin feeling I'm the one to blame

'Cause you dug your own grave, uh huh

After all of the fights and the lies

Yes you wanted to harm me but that won't work anymore

Uh, no more, oh no, it's over

'Cause if it wasn't for all of your torture

I wouldn't know how to be this way now,

and never back down

So I wanna say thank you

(Chorus)

Discuss:

- What kind of situation is talking about that made her stronger?
- Have you ever felt like you were to blame for someone else's bad choices?

Music Lyrics

"Six Feet Tall" by Never Say Never

I met a man of 2 feet tall

this man was quite ambitious

in a world that is so vicious to us all.

I said "hi" as he replied, he said listen to these words

that I have lived by my whole life:

Your only as tall as your heart will let you be,

and your only as small as the world will make you seem.

And when the going gets rough

and you feel like you may fall.

Just look on the bright side, your roughly six feet tall.

I met a man of 12 feet tall, he towered like a giant,

in a world that was defiant of his height.

I said "hi" as he replied, he said listen to these words

that I have dreaded my whole life:

Your only as tall as your heart will let you be,

and your only as small as the world will make you seem.

And when the going gets rough

and you feel like you may fall.

Just look on the bright side, you're roughly six feet tall.

I am a man of six feet tall, just looking for some answers
in a world that answers none of them at all.
I'll say "hi" but no reply to the letters that you write
because I found some piece of mind.

Cause I'm only as tall, as my heart will let me be
and I'm only as small as the world will make me seem.
When the going gets rough, and I feel like I may fall,
I'll look on the bright side, I'm roughly six feet tall

Discuss:

- What do you think this song is about?
- What does it mean to be "as tall as your heart w ll let you be?"
- How could the world make you seem small?

Music Lyrics

"The Climb" by Miley Cyrus

I can almost see it, that dream I'm dreaming,

but there's a voice inside my head saying

You'll never reach it

Every step I'm takin', Every move I make feels

lost with no direction,

My faith is shakin', But I gotta keep tryin',

Gotta keep my head held high

(Chorus)

There's always gonna be another mountain;

I'm always gonna wanna make it move

Always gonna be an uphill battle;

Sometimes I'm gonna have to lose

Ain't about how fast I get there;

Ain't about what's waitin' on the other side;

It's the climb

The struggles I'm facing; The chances I'm taking

Sometimes might knock me down, but No I'm not breaking

I may not know it, but These are the moments that

I'm gonna remember most I've just gotta keep goin', and

I gotta be strong; Just keep pushing on, but

(Chorus 2x)

Keep on movin', Keep climbin', Keep faith baby

It's all about, it's all about the climb

Keep the faith, keep your faith, woah

Discuss:

- What do you think about her saying that it's "gonna be an uphill battle?"
- What does it mean for it to be about the climb, but not about what's waiting on the other side?
- How would people live differently if they believed that life is about the journey rather than what they are going to get when they accomplish whatever?

Music Lyrics

"Barbie Girl" by Aqua

Hi, Barbie!; Hi, Ken!; You wanna go for a ride?;

Sure, Ken!; Jump in!

(Chorus)

I'm a Barbie girl in a Barbie world;

Life in plastic, it's fantastic

You can brush my hair, undress me everywhere

Imagination, life is your creation

Come on Barbie, let's go party!

(Chorus)

I'm a blond bimbo (female) girl in a fantasy world;

Dress me up, make it tight, I'm your dollie

You're my doll, rock'n'roll, feel the glamouring and pain

Kiss me here, touch me there, hanky panky

You can touch, you can play; If you say:

"I'm always yours", ooh wow

(Chorus)

(Loop)

Come on Barbie, let's go party! Ah ah ah yeah

Come on Barbie, let's go party! Ooh wow, ooh wow

Come on Barbie, let's go party! Ah ah ah yeah

Come on Barbie, let's go party! Ooh wow, ooh wcw

Make me walk, make me talk, do whatever you please

I can act like a star, I can beg on my knees

Come jump in, be my friend, let us do it again

Hit the town, fool around, let's go party

You can touch, you can play, If you say:

"I'm always yours" (2x)

(Loop, Chorus 2x, Loop)

Oh, I'm having so much fun!;

Well Barbie, we're just gettin' started;

Oh, I love you Ken!

Discuss:

- Are girls sometimes treated this way?
- How do you think girls feel when they are treated like toys? What can be done about that?
- Who has the power in this relationship? Is this a healthy relationship?

Appendix Contents

Real Girls Survey

Please complete this survey. It contains questions about your view of yourself, media, and your relationships.

Background

Age: ____   Grade: ____

Mother's Education: _____   Father's Education: _____

Live with: __mother only; __father only; __both parents; __other

Typical grades: reading: A, B, C, D, F; math: A, B, C, D, F

Media Literacy

How many **hours** do you spend listening to or watching the following media sources **each day**?

__television; __radio; __CD player/iPod; __Internet

How many hours do you spend talking to family and/or friends
(in person, not on the phone/text/email)? _____

What is your favorite TV show? _____

What is your favorite magazine? _____

What is your favorite movie? _____

What is your favorite website? _____

What is your favorite song? _____

What is your favorite video game? _____

What is your favorite book? _____

Self-Concept

How often are you physically active? ___minutes/day

Do you believe that you are over weight? __yes; __no

Are you currently trying to lose weight? __yes; __no

      If yes, how? __exercise; __diet pills; __fasting;
      __laxatives; __vomiting; __reduced calories

What do you worry about? __being pressured to have sex; __having friends; __fitting in; __being pretty enough; __being smart enough; __graduating from high school

Do you have a boyfriend? __yes; __no

      If yes, how old is he? ___

      Time spent together each week? ___hours

Are your friends sexually active? __yes; __some; __no

Do your friends drink alcohol? __yes; __some; __no

Do your friends use tobacco? __yes; __some; __no

Do your friends use drugs? __yes; __some; __no

Healthy Relationship

How do people treat each other in a healthy relationship?

_____

_____

_____

Please write True or False for the following items.

___It is against my values to have sex before I am married.

___It is against one or both of my parents' values for me to have sex before I am married.

___Teens who have been dating for a long time should have sex if they want to.

Please circle the response that is most like you.

I am happy with who I am.

Never   Sometimes   Often   Always

My friends are smarter or prettier than I am.

Never   Sometimes   Often   Always

I want to look like the girls in magazines.

Never   Sometimes   Often   Always

I compare myself to fashion models.

Never   Sometimes   Often   Always

Women in the media seem like real women.

Never   Sometimes   Often   Always

I let people take advantage of me.

Never   Sometimes   Often   Always

Rubric for Assessing Responses

Level 5

Participant integrates personal feelings, experiences, hopes, fears, reflections, or beliefs with the activity. The personal response is rooted in the activity and a clear understanding of the whole activity, and its connotations, and makes connections to other texts.

Level 4

Participant connects personal feelings, experiences, hopes, fears, reflections, or beliefs with the activity. The personal response refers to the activity, conveys a sense of understanding of the activity and partial understanding of its connotations.

Level 3

Participant explores personal feeling, experiences, hopes, fears, reflections, or beliefs and makes superficial or concrete connections to the activity.

Level 2

Participant retells or paraphrases the activity or identifies aspects in isolation, making only a superficial reference to personal feelings or experiences. Or the participant writes about/discusses personal feelings, etc., without connecting or referring to the activity.

Level 1

Participant response shows little or no interaction with or understanding of the activity.

Level 0

Participant response is irrelevant or incomprehensible.

Group Assessment Chart

You may use the chart below to record individual ratings for each session, based on the rubric. The chart may be copied or recreated to allow for multiple uses. Each girl's name is placed on the left side of the chart. After Session One, use the "1" column to rate the level of participation for each girl. Complete ratings for each girl after every session. There is also a column for rating the Digital Me project or to provide an overall participation rating. Using this chart will allow facilitators to see patterns in participation, as well as individual and group development.

Name	1	2	3	4	5	6	7	8	X

Love the real me or not?

If you look at a situation from more than one angle you can begin to see that things may look different from a different perspective. The same is true for you!

In the stars below, write down things you don't like about your appearance. Then, next to each one, spin the "bad" thing into a good thing by thinking about how it might actually be helpful or good and why you should embrace it.

Real or Reel

Name:

Directions: Think about a television show you have watched that contains a lot of stereotypes.

TV Program Watched:

1. What stereotypes did you see in this show?

2. List a comment or action that illustrated stereotypical thinking.

3. Do you feel that television and media as a whole has an impact on our attitudes and beliefs?

Real People

Have you ever seen or experienced discrimination? When you see the categories below, please list the first message that comes to mind.

An Overweight Girl:

A Poor Girl:

A Teenage Mother:

A Girl Who Attends Private School:

What can you do to when you hear or see people being discriminated against?

Real Conversations

- Can you I cheat from your test because I didn't study?
- You have to tell the teacher that you ruined the textbook, not me.
- I want to borrow your blue shirt to wear to the school party.
- You know, your hair would really look better the other way, you should change it.
- I need to borrow your new sneakers; they will look perfect with my new jeans. I promise I won't ruin them.
- I need to take your car this weekend to go to work.
- Your friend dresses weird; you should stop hanging out with her.

Three Communication Styles

Aggressive: Expressing feelings in a way that violates the rights of others.

Passive: The failure to express needs, opinions, wants.

Assertive: Communicating what you want in a clear, respectful manner.

Real Situations

What would you do? #1

Your friend asks you to come to her house and help her study but what she didn't tell you is that her parents are away on vacation and when you arrive at her home she is having a party instead with alcohol. Which communication style would you use to express your feelings?

What would you do? #2

Your friend says she needs to borrow your new laptop to complete a school project that each of you were given months ago and the project is due in one week. She says that she's been so busy that she hasn't had time to go to the library and use the computers. However, you know that she has been hanging out with her boyfriend almost every day and shopping at the mall with friends after school instead of working on the project. Which communication style would you use to express your feelings?

What would you do? #3

Your boyfriend has been asking you every day during class to leave school early and go hang out at a mutual friend's house. You know that your parents expect you to stay in school and come straight home when school is over. You know if you tell your boyfriend no, he may get upset. Which communication style would you use to express your feelings?

What would you do? #4

Create your own real situation...

Attitude

by: Charles Swindoll

The longer I live, the more I realize the
impact of **attitude** on life.

Attitude, to me, is more important than facts. It is more
important than the past, than education, than money, than
circumstances, than failures, than successes, than what other
people think or say or do. It is more important than appearance,
giftedness or skill. It will make or break a company... a church...
a home.

The remarkable thing is we have a choice every day regarding
the **attitude** we will embrace for that day. We cannot change
our past... we cannot change the fact that people will act in a
certain way. We cannot change the inevitable. The only thing we
can do is play on the one string we have, and that is our
attitude... I am convinced that life is ***10% what happens to
me and
90% how I react to it.***

And so it is with you...
we are in charge of our **attitudes**.

Real Control

Natural Disaster

Having Sex

Cheating

Family

Friends

Grades

Using Drugs

Going to Jail

Joining a Gang

Your School

What Others Think of You

Using Alcohol

Your Future Goals

Power to Say No

Know how you feel ahead of time.

Be firm and repeat what was said.

Be honest.

Speak only for yourself.

Discuss the consequences.

Separate the situation from the person.

Suggest an alternative.

Walk away from the situation.

Boundary Scenarios

Boundary-Crossing Behavior

- When Cheryl walked to class a group of boys whistled at her and it made her feel uncomfortable.
- Ruth keeps texting Christopher asking if he wants to have sex with her. Christopher has a girlfriend and has told Ruth on more than one occasion that he doesn't want to be with her.
- Thomas teased Susan while she was in gym class about her body shape.
- When Sean is at football practice, a group of girls rate how many muscles he has. Sean was so embarrassed.
- Michael never respects the boundaries of the girls in his class. He always gets really close to them and they are always uncomfortable.
- Jack tells Sandra that he will only help her with her project if she has sex with him.

Type of Boundary

- Inappropriate Physical contact
- Non-Consensual sexual advances
- Requests for sexual favors
- Inappropriate Verbal language

Suggested Resources

Movies/Documentaries

PBS Special – *The Merchants of Cool*

http://www.pbs.org/wgbh/pages/frontline/shows/cool/

Mean Girls (2004)

by Mark Waters

Girlhood: Growing up on the inside (2003)

by Liz Garbus

Consuming Kids: The commercialization of childhood (2009)

by Adriana Barbaro

What a Girl Wants (2001)

by Elizabeth Massie

Girls: Moving Beyond Myth (2004)

by Susan MacMillan

Killing Us Softly 4: Advertising's Image of Women (2010)

by Jean Kilbourne

Reviving Ophelia (1998)

by Mary Pipher

Books

Branded - The Buying and Selling of Teenagers
by Alissa Quart

Who's Raising Your Child? - Battling the Marketers for Your Child's Heart and Soul
by Laura J. Buddenberg and Kathleen M. McGee

The Other Parent - The Inside Story of the Media's Effect on Our Children
by James P. Steyer

Made You Look - How Advertising Works and Why You Should Know (for ages 9-12)
by Shari Graydon

Queen Bees & Wannabees
by Rosalind Wiseman

Reviving Ophelia: Saving the selves of adolescent girls
by Mary Pipher

Reaching Teens in Their Natural Habitat
by Danny Holland

Websites

Real Girls – Handouts, surveys, and other tools
http://www.realgirls.us

Tobacco Advertising Gallery: Campaign for Tobacco- Free Kids
http://tobaccofreekids.org/adgallery/

Trinkets & Trash
Artifacts of tobacco industry marketing
http://www.trinketsandtrash.org/

Advertising Avenue
Free archive of commercials for content for advertising analysis.
http://www.advertisementave.com/

The Center on Alcohol Marketing and Youth (CAMY)
http://camy.org/gallery/

About Face
Investigate stereotypes of women found in advertising through galleries of print ads, statistics and activism campaigns.
http://www.about-face.org/

Ad Flips
Archive of "classic" print ads.
http://www.adflip.com/

Adbusters Spoof Ads

Spoofs of popular ads for Tobacco, Alcohol, Food and Fashion.

http://adbusters.org/spoofads/tobacco/

Alliance for a Media Literate America (AMLA)

AMLA is the national membership organization for media literacy.

http://www.AMLAinfo.org

Center for Media Literacy

This organization has set the benchmark for media literacy education.

http://www.medialit.org

New Mexico Media Literacy Project

NMMLP provides current samples of Ads for deconstruction as well as all the basics of media literacy education.

http://www.nmmlp.org/

TV ADS

This website provides a collection of TV ads available for viewing.

http://tvadsview.com

Clip Land

Locate short video clips from commercials, movie trailers, music videos, and short films.

www.clipland.com

References

Adolescent Substance Abuse Knowledge Base. (2007). *Factors of Teen Drug Use.* Retrieved on August 15, 2010 from www.adolescent-substance-abuse.com

American Psychological Association, Task Force on the Sexualization of Girls. (2007). *Report of the APA Task Force on the Sexualization of Girls.* Washington, DC. Retrieved from www.apa.org/pi/wpo/sexualization.html

Ashford, B. (2010). *Taking God to the movies: Nine elements of a Hollywood storyline.* Retrieved on August 18, 2010 from http://betweenthetimes.com/2010/03/10/taking-god-to-the-movies-3-nine-elements-of-a-hollywood-storyline/

Catalano, R., Berglund, L., Ryan J., Lonczak, H., & Hawkins, J. (1998). *Positive youth development in the United States: Research findings on evaluations of positive youth development programs.* Social Development Research Group: University of Washington

Center for Media Literacy. (2007). *5 key questions that can change the world: Lesson plans for media literacy.* Retrieved on August 18, 2010 from http://www.medialit.org/pdf/mlk/02_5KQ_ClassroomGuide.pdf

Centers for Disease Control. (2010). Youth Risk Behavior Surveillance – United States 2009. Retrieved on September

9, 2010 from

http://www.cdc.gov/mmwr/pdf/ss/ss5905.pdf

Centers for Disease Control. (2006). Choose Respect. Retrieved
on August 20, 2010 from

http://www.cdc.gov/chooserespect/about/about.html

Child Development Institute. (2010). *Stages of social-emotional
development in children and teenagers.* Retrieved from

http://www.childdevelopmentinfo.com/development/ericks
on.shtml

Child Welfare League of America. (n.d.). *Communicating with
your teenager.* Retrieved on August 25, 2010 from

http://www.cwla.org/positiveparenting/teen.html

Fabrianesi, B., Jones, S., & Reid, A. (2008). Are pre-adolescent
girls' magazines providing age-appropriate role models?
Health Education, 108(6), 437-449.

Frame, J. (2005). Theology at the movies. Retrieved on
September 4, 2010 from http://www.frame-
poythress.org/frame_books.htm#theologyatthemovies

Girl Scout Research Institute. (2009). Good intentions: The beliefs
and values of teens and tweens today. New York, N.Y., Girl
Scouts of the USA

Girls Incorporated. (2008). *Girls and Violence in the United
States.* Retrieved on August 21, 2010 from

http://www.girlsinc.org/resources/fact-sheets.html

Girls Incorporated. (2002). *Choosing community: Girls get together to be themselves.* Retrieved on August 21, 2010 from http://www.girlsinc.org/resources/fact-sheets.html

Girls Incorporated. (2002). *Girls and media.* Retrieved on August 21, 2010 from http://www.girlsinc.org/resources/fact-sheets.html

Howard, M. (2009). *Media Madness: Get The Rap on the Media.* Atlanta, GA

Kaiser Family Foundation. (2010). *Generation M2: Media in the lives of 8- to 18-year olds.* Menlo, CA

Lemstra, M., Bennett, N., Nannapaneni, U., Newdorf, C., Warren, L., Kershaw, T., & Scott, C. (2010). A systematic review of school-based marijuana and alcohol prevention programs targeting adolescents aged 10–15. *Addiction Research and Theory, 18*(1), 84-96.

Liz Claiborne, Inc. (2010). Troubled Economy Linked to High Levels of Teen Dating Violence & Abuse Survey 2009. Retrieved on September 2, 2010 from http://www.loveisnotabuse.com/web/guest/survey2009

Love, Inc. (2010). Sound off for poverty. Retrieved on September 9, 2010 from http://www.soundoffforpoverty.org/

Malekoff, A. (2004). *Strengths-based group work with children and adolescents. Handbook of social work with groups.* New York: Guildford Press, 227-244.

McDonnell, J. (1992). *Christian discernment in a mass –mediated culture.* Retrieved from http://www.medialit.org/reading_room/article587.html

Media Literacy Project. (2010). *The language of persuasion.* Retrieved on September 3, 2010 from http://www.nmmlp.org/media_literacy/pdfs/Language_of_Persuasion.pdf

Middleman, R., & Goldberg Wood, G. (1990). *Skills for direct practice in social work.* New York, N.Y.: Columbia University Press.

Primack, B., Dalton, M., Carroll, M., Agarwal, A., Fine, M. (2008). Content Analysis of Tobacco, Alcohol, and Other Drugs in Popular Music. *Arch Pediatr Adolesc Med, 162* (2), 169-175.

Steyn, D. (2006). *Screening the screen: Media literacy and the christian.* Retrieved on September 9, 2010 from http://dialogue.adventist.org/articles/17_3_steyn_ep.htm

The Dove Self Esteem Fund. (2008). *Real girls, real pressure: A national report on the state of self-esteem.*

The Medical Institute for Sexual Health. (2005). *Questions kids ask about sex: Honest answers for every age.* Grand Rapics, MI: Baker Publishing Group.

Tuckman, B. & Jensen, M. (1977). Stages of small-group development revisted. *Group & Organization Management, 2*(4), 419-427.

About the Authors

Jessica Traylor has extensive experience and training in youth development, group facilitation, program planning, culturally relevant teaching practices, statistical research, data analysis, parent engagement, and staff development. Mrs. Traylor was a featured presenter at national conferences, including: The National Youth at Risk Conference; The National Association of Social Workers Conference, Georgia Chapter. Jessica earned a B.S. in Psychology with a minor in Sociology from Georgia State University, followed by a M.Ed. and Ed.S in School Psychology from Georgia Southern University. Mrs. Traylor began her career in education as a Special Education Teacher. Currently, Jessica is a School Psychologist in Central Georgia. Jessica resides in Milner, GA with her husband and two children.

Kiana Clayborn has practiced as a Licensed Master Social Worker in both New York and Georgia. Her practice areas include school social work, case management, advocacy, program planning, youth development, group work, parent engagement, and staff development. Ms. Clayborn has been a featured presenter at national conferences, including: The National Youth At Risk Conference and The National Association of Social Workers Conference, Georgia Chapter. Kiana received both her B.A. degree in Sociology and her M.S.W. degree in Social Welfare from the State University of New York at Stony Brook. Ms. Clayborn began her career as a Social Work Case Manager in Preventive Services. Currently, she is a School Social Worker in Central Georgia.

www.ingramcontent.com/pod-product-compliance
Lightning Source LLC
LaVergne TN
LVHW021504080426
835509LV00018B/2400